Contents

Contents

Name _____

Person to Person

The characters in this theme learn about themselves and others. After reading each story, complete the chart below to show what you have learned about the characters. **(10 points per selection)**

	Mariah Keeps Cool	**Mom's Best Friend**
Who is the main character or characters?	Mariah **(2 points)**	Mom and her daughter, the narrator. **(2)**
How do the story characters try to help each other?	Mariah throws a surprise party for her sister Lynn. The guests help by bringing gifts for the homeless shelter where Lynn volunteers. **(2)**	The family helps Mom by taking care of the house while Mom is away learning how to work with her new dog guide. **(2)**
How do the story characters communicate with each other?	The characters spend a lot of time talking together and planning for the party. **(2)**	The narrator and Mom write letters back and forth. Also, Mom communicates with her dog guide through words and gestures. **(2)**

Assessment Tip: Total **6** points per selection and **2** points for the final question

Name _____

Person to Person continued

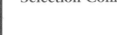

	Yang the Second and Her Secret Admirers	Dear Mr. Henshaw
Who is the main character or characters?	Yingtao and Yinglan, or Second Sister (2)	Leigh Botts (2)
How do the story characters try to help each other?	Yingtao and his sister try to help Second Sister feel more at home in America by matching her up with Paul Eng, a boy from school. (2)	Angela Badger tries to encourage students to be better writers. (2)
How do the story characters communicate with each other?	The characters talk to each other. Yingtao and his sister stage conversations for Second Sister and Paul. (2)	Leigh writes letters to Mr. Henshaw. The characters also talk to each other. (2)

What have you learned about working together in this theme?

Sample answer: There are many ways people can work together. _____

Communication exists in many forms. (2) _____

_____

Assessment Tip: Total **6** points per selection and **2** points for the final question

Name _____

Guests of Honor

Answer each of the following questions by writing a vocabulary word.

1. Which word means "make something look nice"?
   decorate **(1 point)**

2. Which word tells what people do when they stop someone and delay him or her for a while? detain **(1)**

3. Which word means "people who make up an audience"?
   spectators **(1)**

4. Which word means "express a willingness to help"?
   volunteer **(1)**

5. Which word describes an event with lively music and colorful decorations? festive **(1)**

6. Which word is another word for *party*? celebration **(1)**

7. Which word means "unwilling"? reluctant **(1)**

8. Which word has the same meaning as *astonishingly*?
   amazingly **(1)**

9. Which word means "believes something is wrong"?
   suspects **(1)**

10. Which word means "to show respect for someone publicly"?
    honor **(1)**

Now write the first letter of each of the last five words you wrote above to answer this question.

What noise might tip off a person that he or she is about to be surprised? crash **(2)**

Name _____

This Was Their Solution!

Read the problem stated in the left-hand column. Fill in the Solution column with information from the selection.

Problem	Solution
Lynn overhears Mariah say "See you later" to Denise and is curious about why they were going to be together.	Mariah tells Lynn that <u>she is</u> <u>going to see Denise when she</u> <u>gets back home.</u> **(2 points)**
Lynn shows up unexpectedly at Brandon's house while they're making decorations.	Mariah, Brandon, and the girls <u>convince Lynn that she cannot</u> <u>stay to watch.</u> **(2)**
Lynn doesn't want a birthday celebration; she just wants to stay in bed all day.	Mariah asks her mother to <u>take</u> <u>Lynn to the bookstore to get her</u> <u>out of the house.</u> **(2)**.
Mariah forgets to get music for the party.	Mariah's father calls Brandon's father because <u>he has music</u> <u>equipment he can bring over.</u> **(2)**
Mariah and the rest of the Friendly Five don't have anyone to dance with.	Mariah suggests that they <u>dance</u> <u>together, or by themselves.</u> **(2)**

Assessment Tip: Total **10** Points

Name _____

Surprise Party Advice

Based on what you've learned from the selection, complete the sentences below giving advice about how to throw a successful surprise party. (Answers will vary.)

▶ On the party invitations, make sure everyone knows <u>that the party is a surprise,</u> <u>when and where it is taking place, and any other special instructions about</u> <u>what to bring or do.</u> **(1 point)**

▶ Speak carefully when you're around the guest of honor, so <u>you don't accidentally</u> <u>give away the surprise.</u> **(1)**

▶ If you say something that makes the guest of honor suspicious, be ready to tell a story that <u>gives another explanation for what you've said.</u> **(1)**

_____

▶ A few days before the party, get others to help you <u>make party decorations.</u> **(1)**

▶ If the guest of honor unexpectedly appears while party preparations are taking place, figure out <u>another way to explain what is going on.</u> **(1)**

▶ On the day of the party, ask others to help you <u>set up for the party.</u> **(1)**

_____

▶ If the party is taking place at the guest of honor's house, ask someone to <u>get that person out of the house while you set up the party.</u> **(1)**

▶ Be sure to have plenty of <u>food and drinks **(1)**</u> available for your guests.

▶ If you want to have music at the party, be sure that you have <u>all the musical</u> <u>equipment you will need.</u> **(1)**

▶ And remember to <u>have fun **(1)**</u> yourself!

Name _____

Think It Through

Read the passage.   Then complete the activity on page 7.

Munching on Leaves

Julie's little brother Pablo was obsessed with the movie *Bugs*. This wouldn't have been a problem, except that Aunt Elena bought him the soundtrack, and Pablo listened to it nonstop, especially one song called "The Caterpillar Crawl." The chorus went: "Merrily we crawl along, crawl along, munchin' leaves all day!" It had one of those catchy tunes that sticks in your mind even though it is the last song in the world that you want to sing. Last week Julie's friend Diana had looked at her strangely and asked, "What are you singing? Something about munching *leaves*?" Julie knew she had to do something.

"I can't listen to that CD anymore," she told her father. "Not one more time. If I hear it one more time, I will scream."

Dad sighed. "Yes, I know," he said. "Yesterday at the office I started singing 'Don't Bug Me' during a meeting."

"Can't you tell him not to play it anymore?"

"Well, would it be fair if I told you not to play one of your CDs?"

"It would be if I played one CD over and over and over again."

"What about the time I asked you to stop playing that Screaming Purple Rhinos CD?" Julie could see that her dad had a point.

She went to the library and searched until she found an audiotape of folk songs that she had loved when she was six. She checked it out, brought it home, and started playing it on her own tape player. When Pablo asked what it was, she said, "Never mind," and shut her door.

Soon she heard him tapping. "Can't I listen to that?"

"No, it's mine. Go listen to your *Bugs* CD." She heard him complaining to Dad. Julie came out of her room and said, "Oh, all right. You can listen to it, but you have to give it back right afterwards." Of course, he didn't, which had been her plan all along.

By the time Julie was sick of the folk song tape, it was due back at the library.

Name _____

Think It Through continued

Answer these questions about the passage on page 6.

Answers may vary. Sample answers shown.

1. What problem does Julie have in the story? She is sick of the CD her little brother keeps playing again and again. **(3 points)**

2. What solution does Julie think of first? She asks her dad to tell Pablo not to play the CD anymore. **(3)**

3. After thinking about that solution, what does Julie decide? She decides that it's not really fair to ask Pablo to stop listening to the CD. **(3)**

4. What solution does she think of next? She draws Pablo's attention to a recording of folk songs she used to like, so that he forgets about the *Bugs* CD. **(3)**

5. Do you think her solution is a good one? Why or why not? Yes. It solves the problem without being unfair or making Pablo feel bad. **(3)**

6. Think about the steps to solving a problem. Which steps did Julie follow, and how well did she follow them? First, she identified the problem. Then, she thought about different solutions. Finally, she picked the best solution and followed through on it. Julie did a good job of following the steps. **(3)**

Name _____

Divide and Define

Read each sentence. Rewrite the underlined word with a slash (/) to divide the syllables. Then, after it, write a definition or synonym for the word. Sample answers shown. Accept all reasonable definitions.

1. As you <u>approach</u> the yard, you will smell the hot dogs.

   ap/proach; to come near **(2 points)**

2. I'll be ready for the party in an <u>instant</u>.

   in/stant; moment **(2)**

3. Lynn is always <u>hungry</u> when she wakes up in the morning.

   hun/gry; starved **(2)**

4. I'll call you when the decorations are <u>complete</u>.

   com/plete; finished **(2)**

5. On his vacation in Maine, Brendan went out on a <u>lobster</u> boat.

   lob/ster; a sea animal **(2)**

6. Will you please <u>increase</u> the volume on the CD player?

   in/crease; make greater **(2)**

7. Mariah decided to <u>confront</u> Denise about the rumor she had heard.

   con/front; meet face to face **(2)**

8. The balloons and colored paper make a beautiful <u>display</u>.

   dis/play; exhibit **(2)**

Assessment Tip: Total **16** Points

Name _____

VCCCV Pattern

Two-syllable words with the VCCCV pattern have two consonants that spell one sound, as in *laughter*, or that form a cluster, as in *complain*. Divide a VCCCV word into syllables before or after those consonants. Then look for familiar patterns that you have learned, and spell the word by syllables.

VCC | CV   **laugh | ter**   VC | CCV   **com | plain**

Write each Spelling Word under the heading that shows where it is divided. Order of answers for each category may vary.

VC | CCV

district **(1 point)**   mischief **(1)**

address **(1)**   complex **(1)**

complain **(1)**   orphan **(1)**

explain **(1)**   constant **(1)**

improve **(1)**   dolphin **(1)**

farther **(1)**   employ **(1)**

simply **(1)**   monster **(1)**

hundred **(1)**   orchard **(1)**

although **(1)**

VCC | CV

laughter **(1)**   sandwich **(1)**

partner **(1)**

Name _____

Spelling Spree

Syllable Addition **Combine the first syllable of the first word with the final syllable of the second word to write a Spelling Word.**

1. addition + headdress = _____
2. parting + runner = _____
3. monsoon + youngster = _____
4. farsighted + father = _____
5. command + floodplain = _____
6. concern + instant = _____
7. empire + deploy = _____

1. address (**1 point**)
2. partner (**1**)
3. monster (**1**)
4. farther (**1**)

5. complain (**1**)
6. constant (**1**)
7. employ (**1**)

Word Clues **Write a Spelling Word to fit each clue.**

8. a child whose parents have died
9. two pieces of bread and a slice of cheese
10. an area set aside for a specific purpose
11. where you can find apple trees
12. a reaction to a joke
13. an aquatic mammal
14. a word meaning "even though"

8. orphan (**1**)
9. sandwich (**1**)
10. district (**1**)
11. orchard (**1**)

12. laughter (**1**)
13. dolphin (**1**)
14. although (**1**)

Spelling Words

1. district
2. address
3. complain
4. explain
5. improve
6. farther
7. simply
8. hundred
9. although
10. laughter
11. mischief
12. complex
13. partner
14. orphan
15. constant
16. dolphin
17. employ
18. sandwich
19. monster
20. orchard

Assessment Tip: Total **14** Points

Name _____

Proofreading and Writing

Circle the six misspelled Spelling Words in this birthday card that Mariah might have sent. Then write each word correctly.

Dear Lynn,

Let me (explane) why we threw you a surprise party. It wasn't to create (mischeif.) Although you said you (simplie) wanted to stay in bed on your birthday, we had to show how much we care about you. That's why we decided on something more (complecks) than a simple party. By having the guests bring things for your friends at the shelter, we might be able to (improve) the lives of the people there. I hope it's the best party you'll ever have, even if you live to be a (hunderd!)

Your loving sister,
Mariah

1. district
2. address
3. complain
4. explain
5. improve
6. farther
7. simply
8. hundred
9. although
10. laughter
11. mischief
12. complex
13. partner
14. orphan
15. constant
16. dolphin
17. employ
18. sandwich
19. monster
20. orchard

1. explain **(1 point)**

2. mischief **(1)**

3. simply **(1)**

4. complex **(1)**

5. improve **(1)**

6. hundred **(1)**

✏️— **Write About an Experience** Have you ever worked together with your family or friends to surprise someone? What was the surprise? How did you organize it? Were you able to keep it a secret until the end? How did the person being surprised react?

On a separate piece of paper, write a paragraph describing the experience. Use Spelling Words from the list. Responses will vary. **(4)**

Assessment Tip: Total **10** Points

Name _____

Inflection Connection

**Read each word and its definition. Pay attention to inflected endings
such as -s, -es, -ed, -ing, -er, -est. Then use inflected forms of each
word to complete the sentences below.**

> *dance* (dăns) *v.* danced, dancing, dances. To move in time to music.
>
> *happy* (hăp´ ē) *adj.* happier, happiest. Showing or feeling joy or pleasure.
>
> *noisy* (noi´ zē) *adj.* noisier, noisiest. Full of or accompanied by noise.
>
> *party* (pär´ tē) *n.*, pl. parties. A social gathering for pleasure or entertainment.
>
> *supply* (sə plī´) *v.* supplied, supplying, supplies. To make available for
>   use; provide.

1. Everyone agreed that Rosa's birthday celebration was one of the

    best <u>parties **(2 points)**</u> they had been to.

2. Gabe shouted to Danny that he had never been to a

    <u>noisier **(2)**</u> party.

3. Conchita <u>supplied **(2)**</u> the music from her large CD
    collection.

4. Singing and <u>dancing **(2)**</u> went on late into the night.

5. Rosa's big smile showed that she was the <u>happiest **(2)**</u>
    person there.

Assessment Tip: Total **10** Points

Name _____

Strong, Stronger, Strongest

Comparing with Adjectives Add -er to most adjectives to compare two people, places, or things. Use *more* with long adjectives to compare two items. Add -est to most adjectives to compare three or more. Use *most* with long adjectives to compare three or more.

1. **Most Adjectives**
   Add -er or -est to the adjective.

   Tanya is strong.
   Chris is **stronger** than Tanya.
   Pat is the **strongest** of all.

2. **Adjectives with Two or More Syllables**
   Use *more* or *most*.

   It is a beautiful view.
   It is a **more beautiful** view from here.
   It is the **most beautiful** view of all.

Complete each sentence with the correct form of the adjective in parentheses.

1. She is the <u>most generous **(1 point)**</u> person I know. (generous)

2. Denise is a <u>more skillful **(1)**</u> artist than I am. (skillful)

3. Her mother was the <u>calmest **(1)**</u> one there. (calm)

4. It was the <u>greatest **(1)**</u> night of the year. (great)

5. I'd like a <u>smaller **(1)**</u> slice of cake than that, please. (small)

6. LaToya is the <u>kindest **(1)**</u> person I know. (kind)

7. Of all our houses, Marco's house is the <u>nearest **(1)**</u> one to the school. (near)

8. Marsha is a <u>more talented **(1)**</u> singer than Carlos. (talented)

9. However, Carlos is the <u>most gifted **(1)**</u> bass player in the school. (gifted)

10. I am a <u>faster **(1)**</u> reader than a writer. (fast)

Name _____

'Tis Better to Give Than to Receive

Comparing with *good* and *bad* The adjectives *good* and *bad* have irregular comparative forms. Use *better* to compare two things, and *best* to compare three or more. Use *worse* to compare two things, and *worst* to compare three or more.

	Good	**Bad**
Comparing two	This lunch is **better** than yesterday's.	I did **worse** on this test than the last one.
Comparing three or more	It is the **best** lunch I've ever had.	In fact, this is the **worst** I've ever done.

Fill in each blank with the correct form of *good* or *bad*. Answers may vary.

1. Donating used clothing is a <u>better **(1 point)**</u> act than throwing it away.

2. In fact, it is probably the <u>best **(1)**</u> thing you can do with old clothing.

3. Icy sidewalks are a <u>worse **(1)**</u> hazard for frail people than for others.

4. Last winter was the <u>worst **(1)**</u> winter on record.

5. Hooray! This month's food drive was a <u>better **(1)**</u> one than last month's.

6. In fact, it was the <u>best **(1)**</u> food drive we've ever had.

7. What is the <u>worst/best **(1)**</u> thing that has ever happened to you?

8. Uncle Sal has a <u>better **(1)**</u> garden than my mother.

9. In fact, he won an award for the <u>best **(1)**</u> garden in the neighborhood.

10. She has a <u>worse **(1)**</u> cold than I had.

Assessment Tip: Total **10** Points

Name _____

Lighter and Warmer

Combining Sentences with Adjectives To avoid having too many short, comparing sentences, you can combine sentences to make one sentence with two or more comparative adjectives. Here is an example:

Two sentences: This year's swim team is **more enthusiastic** than last year's team. It is a **stronger** team too.

One sentence: This year's swim team is **more enthusiastic and stronger** than last year's team.

Mark wrote a draft of an article for the school paper. Revise the five underlined pairs of sentences by combining them to form sentences with more than one comparative adjective.

I am a member of the swim team. Being on the team has given me a busier life. It has given me a better life too. I get up at 6 A.M. for practice. In the winter, it was darker outside than it had been in the fall. It was colder too. That was hard, but when I got to school I saw my teammates. Pat would tell funny jokes. Dale would tell even funnier jokes. Dale told sillier jokes too.

Now that spring is here, warmer days have arrived. Lighter days have arrived too. It is easy to practice a lot when it is light. We will have a stronger team for our next meet. We will have a faster team too. I love to swim, but the best part of being on the team is working with great friends.

1. Being on the team has given me a busier and better life. **(2 points)**

2. In the winter, it was darker and colder outside than it had been in the fall. **(2)**

3. Dale would tell even funnier and sillier jokes. **(2)**

4. Now that spring is here, warmer and lighter days have arrived. **(2)**

5. We will have a stronger and faster team for our next meet. **(2)**

Writing a Memo

A **memo** is a brief, informal message sent from one person to others in the same company, group, or organization. Sometimes people write memos to each other when they work together as a team.

Use this page to plan a memo to your classmates or other students at school about an important event. Follow these steps:

▶ **Name the person or the persons to whom you are writing.**

▶ **Tell who is writing the memo.**

▶ **Write the date.**

▶ **Identify the subject of the memo.**

▶ **Write the body of the memo. Begin by stating why you are writing. Use clear, direct language and a businesslike tone. Be brief but include all the important information. If you want a response, end by asking a question or by requesting an action.**

MEMORANDUM

To: (2 points) _____

From: (2) _____

Date: (2) _____

Subject: (2) _____

(4) _____

_____

_____

_____

_____

When you finish your memo, check it for correct grammar and punctuation and for complete sentences. Then copy your memo on a clean sheet of paper and post it or send it.

Assessment Tip: Total **12** Points

Name _____

Changing Positions of Adjectives

An **adjective** describes a noun or pronoun. Adjectives may come before or after the nouns or pronouns they describe. Good writers place adjectives in different positions in a sentence to add variety to their writing.

First, circle the adjectives in the following memo from Denise to the other party organizers. Then rewrite the body of the memo on the lines, changing the positions of some adjectives to add variety. Either place the adjectives before or after the nouns they describe.

(1 point for each adjective)

To: All Party Organizers

From: Denise

Date: July 15

Subject: Surprise Party Decorations

We will meet at Brandon's house on Wednesday, July 18, at 1 P.M. We will create decorations that are (pretty) yet (inexpensive) Bring scissors to make flowers that are (paper,) signs that are (handmade,) and banners that are (long) and (colorful.) Sometimes decorations that are (simple) and (easy) to make are the most effective. I know the backyard will look like a garden that is (beautiful.) Lynn and the other guests will be (happy!)

Responses will vary. **(10)**

We will meet at Brandon's house on Wednesday, July 18, at 1 P.M. We will create

decorations that are pretty yet inexpensive. Bring scissors to make paper flowers,

handmade signs, and long, colorful banners. Sometimes decorations that are

simple and easy to make are the most effective. I know the backyard will look like a

beautiful garden. Lynn and the other guests will be happy!

Name _____

Revising Your Personal Narrative

Reread your personal narrative. Put a checkmark in the box for each sentence that describes your paper. Use this page to help you revise.

Rings the Bell

☐ My story starts with an attention-grabbing beginning.

☐ All events are focused on a single experience. They are also told in order. I used time-order words.

☐ Details, exact words, and dialogue bring my story to life.

☐ You can tell how I felt. My writing sounds like me.

☐ My narrative has sentence variety. There are almost no mistakes.

Getting Stronger

☐ The beginning could be more interesting.

☐ Some details don't relate to the topic. Some events are out of order.

☐ I should add details, exact words, and dialogue.

☐ My voice could be stronger. I could have made my feelings clearer.

☐ My sentences need some more variety. There are some mistakes.

Try Harder

☐ The beginning is missing or weak.

☐ The narrative is not focused. The order is unclear.

☐ There are almost no details or exact words.

☐ I can't hear my voice at all. I didn't write about how I felt.

☐ There is no sentence variety. Mistakes make it hard to read.

Name _____

Varying Sentence Types

Read the paragraph. All the sentences are declarative sentences.

Yesterday I had a bad day. I overslept. I didn't have time for breakfast. I missed the bus. I yelled at it to stop. It was too late. No one heard me. I walked all the way to school. I wondered what I had done to deserve this. I was late, and I didn't have a note from my mom. The day went downhill from there.

Now rewrite the paragraph, varying the sentence types. Include at least one question, one exclamation, and one command. You will need to add or delete words to revise the sentences.

Answers will vary. **(10 points)**

_____

_____

_____

_____

_____

_____

_____

_____

_____

_____

_____

_____

Name _____

Spelling Words

Words Often Misspelled Look for familiar spelling patterns to help you remember how to spell the Spelling Words on this page. Think carefully about the parts that you find hard to spell in each word.

Write the missing letters in the Spelling Words below.
Order of answers for 12–13 may vary.

1. <u>a</u>_____ lot (**1 point**)

2. bec <u>a</u>_____ <u>u</u>_____ se (**1**)

3. s <u>c</u>_____ <u>h</u>_____ ool (**1**)

4. it <u>s</u>_____ (**1**)

5. it '_____ <u>s</u>_____ (**1**)

6. ton <u>i</u>_____ <u>g</u>_____ <u>h</u>_____ t (**1**)

7. m <u>i</u>_____ <u>g</u>_____ <u>h</u>_____ t (**1**)

8. r <u>i</u>_____ <u>g</u>_____ <u>h</u>_____ t (**1**)

9. <u>w</u>_____ <u>r</u>_____ ite (**1**)

10. ag <u>a</u>_____ <u>i</u>_____ n (**1**)

11. t <u>o</u>_____ (**1**)

12. t <u>o</u>_____ <u>o</u>_____ (**1**)

13. t <u>w</u>_____ <u>o</u>_____ (**1**)

14. th <u>e</u>_____ <u>y</u>_____ (**1**)

15. tha <u>t</u>_____ '_____ <u>s</u>_____ (**1**)

Spelling Words

1. a lot
2. because
3. school
4. its
5. it's
6. tonight
7. might
8. right
9. write
10. again
11. to
12. too
13. two
14. they
15. that's

Study List On a separate piece of paper, write each Spelling Word. Check your spelling against the words on the list.
Order of words may vary. (**5**)

Spelling Spree

Homophone Blanks The blanks in each of the following sentences can be filled with homophones from the Spelling Word list. Write the words in the correct order.

1-2. I think _____ too bad that the park lost the funding for _____ swimming pool.

3-5. The _____ football players decided that they would try _____ play on the basketball team, _____.

6-7. After she broke her arm, Leslie couldn't _____ with her _____ hand.

1-2. it's **(1 point)**   its **(1)**

3-5. two **(1)**   to **(1)**   too **(1)**

6-7. write **(1)**   right **(1)**

Crack the Code Some Spelling Words have been written in the code below. Use the code to figure out each word. Then write the words correctly.

CODE:	B	P	Y	L	A	T	R	F	D	W	Z	X	V	I	O
LETTER:	a	b	c	e	g	h	i	l	m	n	o	s	t	u	y

8. DRATV   8. might **(1)**

9. B FZV   9. a lot **(1)**

10. XYTZZF   10. school **(1)**

11. VTBV'X   11. that's **(1)**

12. BABRW   12. again **(1)**

13. VTLO   13. they **(1)**

14. PLYBIXL   14. because **(1)**

15. VZWRATV   15. tonight **(1)**

Spelling Words

1. a lot
2. because
3. school
4. its
5. it's
6. tonight
7. might
8. right
9. write
10. again
11. to
12. too
13. two
14. they
15. that's

Assessment Tip: Total **15** Points

Name _____

Proofreading and Writing

Proofreading Circle the five misspelled Spelling Words in this advertisement. Then write each word correctly.

Has it been (two) long since you talked to your best friend? Do you feel like you don't have the time to (wright) to the people you care about? Then (its) time to call them, person to person! There's nothing like a conversation to get you back in touch. And it doesn't cost (alot,) either! Call (tonite)— you'll be glad you did.

1. a lot
2. because
3. school
4. its
5. it's
6. tonight
7. might
8. right
9. write
10. again
11. to
12. too
13. two
14. they
15. that's

1. too **(1 point)**

2. write **(1)**

3. it's **(1)**

4. a lot **(1)**

5. tonight **(1)**

▬▬▬ **Write a Conversation** Work with one or more classmates to create a conversation. One person writes a sentence, using a Spelling Word, to open the conversation. The next person writes the second sentence, using a Spelling Word. From here, take turns writing sentences, using Spelling Words from the list. Responses will vary. **(5)**

Assessment Tip: Total **10** Points

Name _____

A Friend and a Helper

Use words from the box to complete the paragraphs below.

A person who cannot see may use a <u>dog guide **(1 point)**</u> as a helper when going from place to place. In order to do this important work, a dog must go through <u>obedience **(1)**</u> training. It must learn to ignore its <u>instinct **(1)**</u> to chase other dogs. It must also learn to help its master avoid <u>obstacles **(1)**</u> and cross streets safely. Only a <u>mature **(1)**</u> dog can be trained effectively. Once a dog has <u>mastered **(1)**</u> the basic skills, it can go to live with its master and begin developing an <u>attachment **(1)**</u> to that person.

Dogs are helpful in a number of ways, but people who cannot see still must spend time <u>memorizing **(1)**</u> the <u>layout **(1)**</u> of a building in which they will be spending time. They also must depend on their listening skills and their ability to read <u>braille **(1)**</u> in order to acquire new knowledge and be more independent.

Name _____

Tell Me All the Details!

Look for details in the selection, and fill in each Details column. Read
the prompts in the far left-hand column to determine if the details belong
before, while, or *after* Mom went to The Seeing Eye. Sample details shown.

	Details about Mom	Details about Narrator	Details about Ursula
Before Mom returns to The Seeing Eye	she's blind; misses Marit has sensitive hearing **(1 point)**	**(1)**	**(1)**
While Mom is at The Seeing Eye	**(1)**	misses Mom; divided house chores; wonders if she'll love Ursula **(1)**	sprang up on the narrator; every day learned one route in the neighborhood **(1)**
After Mom returns from The Seeing Eye	**(1)**	**(1)**	started "loneliness training" **(1)**

Write one sentence with details about The Seeing Eye.

(1) _____

_____

Assessment Tip: Total **10** Points

Name _____

Trace the "Route" of the Selection

Complete the sentences in the boxes below to show the steps in Ursula's training process. Sample answers are shown.

1. Mom returns to
   The Seeing Eye training
   school in Morristown,
   New Jersey **(2 points)**
   where she gets her new guide
   dog, Ursula.

2. After making mistakes in her early lessons, Ursula
   starts to get better at
   guiding Mom. **(2)**

3. In addition to training with Ursula, Mom spends her time at The Seeing Eye
   talking with her new
   blind friends. **(2)**

4. When Mom brings Ursula home, she continues
   her training by teaching
   Ursula new routes and
   giving her obedience
   lessons. **(2)**

5. When Ursula finally feels comfortable in her new home,
   Mom starts _loneliness_
   training **(2)**

6. Ursula soon becomes
   a beloved and important
   part of Mom's family. **(2)**

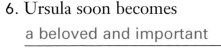

Reading Carefully

Read the passage. Then complete the activity on page 27.

Louis Braille

Louis Braille was born in France in 1809. At the age of three, he had an accident in his father's workshop and became blind. His father wanted young Louis to become educated and successful, so he enrolled Louis in the Royal Institute for Blind Youth in Paris when Louis was ten years old. The Institute was a school that specialized in teaching blind students.

Louis proved himself to be an outstanding student. He learned to read, though books for people who were blind were rare and hard to use at that time. The Institute had only three books in its library. Each book was divided into twenty parts, and each part weighed more than twenty pounds. A person read the text by touching the huge raised letters on each page.

Shortly after Louis came to the Institute, a military officer named Charles Barbier brought his own system of writing to the attention of the school. He had invented a system he called "night writing." It consisted of raised dots and dashes on thin cardboard and was used by night watchmen to send and receive messages. Louis was fascinated with the system, and he decided to try to improve it.

Louis worked day and night. He used only the dots and found that a "cell" made up of up to six dots could be changed to form sixty-three different patterns. Using his six-dot cell, Louis made a separate pattern for each letter of the alphabet, for numbers, punctuation marks, and even musical notes. This system, which became known as *braille*, is used in countries throughout the world.

Name _____

Reading Carefully continued

Read each statement below. Write a detail from the passage on page 26 to support the statement. Sample answers shown.

Conclusions	Supporting Details
1. Louis was intelligent and hard-working.	1. He proved himself to be an outstanding student. **(3 points)**
2. Louis had sensitive fingers and could learn new things.	2. He learned to read through touch. **(3)**
3. Before the invention of braille, books for people who were blind were hard to read.	3. These books were rare, hard to use, and heavy. **(3)**
4. Louis was creative and liked to try new things.	4. He helped invent a new way of writing. **(3)**
5. Louis was patient and determined.	5. He worked day and night to find the six-dot system. **(3)**
6. The invention of braille affects the lives of many people.	6. Braille is used in countries throughout the world. **(3)**

Viva Vowels!

Read the letter. Notice that each underlined word has two vowels with the VV pattern. If the vowels should be kept together in a syllable, circle the vowels. If the vowels should be divided between syllables, draw a line between the vowels. Two examples have been done for you. (1 point each)

actual

believer

pause

create

complains

librarian

laziest

Dear kids,

Today could not have been much crazier! I spent so much time with Prince, my dog guide, that both of us were exhausted. And Prince still had to see the veterinarian.

I can't wait for you to meet Prince. He is a golden retriever. I wish I could explain to him what our routine at home will usually involve. I do not think he realizes that he is soon going to end his training.

Love, Mom

Now use the VV words in the word box to complete these sentences.

1. After a short __pause (1)__ for a sip of water, the speaker continued.

2. The __librarian (1)__ told me that the latest *Billy Burton* mystery just came in!

3. "You are the __laziest (1)__ animal I've ever known," I said to my sleeping cat.

4. I didn't think you could win the race, but you've made me a __believer (1)__.

5. Our neighbor __complains (1)__ that the garbage collector comes too early in the morning.

6. This is not a copy of the Gilroy diamond; it is the __actual (1)__ jewel!

7. I asked the puppeteer how she was able to __create (1)__ such lifelike puppets.

Assessment Tip: Total **12** Points

Name _____

VV Pattern

When the two vowels in a VV pattern spell two vowel sounds, divide the word into syllables between the vowels. Look for familiar patterns that you have learned, and spell the word by syllables.

V | V   V | V

po | em   cre | ate

► The word *quiet* has three vowels that appear together. In this word, the *u* goes with *q* to make the consonant sound /kw/.

Write each Spelling Word. Draw a line between the two vowels in each VV syllable pattern. Order of answers may vary.

V | V

po | em **(1 point)**	di | et **(1)**
ide | a **(1)**	li | ar **(1)**
cre | ate **(1)**	fu | el **(1)**
di | ary **(1)**	ri | ot **(1)**
are | a **(1)**	actu | al **(1)**
gi | ant **(1)**	li | on **(1)**
usu | al **(1)**	ru | in **(1)**
radi | o **(1)**	tri | al **(1)**
cru | el **(1)**	rode | o **(1)**
qui | et **(1)**	sci | ence **(1)**

Spelling Words

1. poem
2. idea
3. create
4. diary
5. area
6. giant
7. usual
8. radio
9. cruel
10. quiet*
11. diet
12. liar
13. fuel
14. riot
15. actual
16. lion
17. ruin
18. trial
19. rodeo
20. science

Name _____

Spelling Spree

Phrase Fillers Write the Spelling Word that best completes each phrase.

1. a nutritious, low-fat _____

2. to call an untruthful person a _____

3. a _____ by jury

4. the _____ of biology

5. a _____ with four verses

6. an ancient, crumbling _____

7. a fairy tale with a towering _____

8. the mane of a _____

9. an _____ for a new product

1. diet **(1 point)**
2. liar **(1)**
3. trial **(1)**
4. science **(1)**
5. poem **(1)**

6. ruin **(1)**
7. giant **(1)**
8. lion **(1)**
9. idea **(1)**

1. poem
2. idea
3. create
4. diary
5. area
6. giant
7. usual
8. radio
9. cruel
10. quiet*
11. diet
12. liar
13. fuel
14. riot
15. actual
16. lion
17. ruin
18. trial
19. rodeo
20. science

Syllable Scramble Rearrange the syllables to write a Spelling Word. One syllable in each item is extra.

Example: ish ble fin   *finish*

10. ra dis o di   radio **(1)**

11. al u ent su   usual **(1)**

12. ru ot ri   riot **(1)**

13. a di sci ry   diary **(1)**

14. tu re ac al   actual **(1)**

15. de o ro ant   rodeo **(1)**

Assessment Tip: Total **15** Points

Name _____

Proofreading and Writing

Proofreading Circle the five misspelled Spelling Words in this set of guidelines. Then write each word correctly.

Tips on Caring for Your New Dog Guide

1. Be sure to (creat) a comfortable home environment for your dog. A calm and (quiete) atmosphere is best.

2. Feed your dog a healthy diet. Just as food gives you energy, a dog's food is its (fule) too.

3. Discipline your dog firmly but kindly.

4. Never be (crual) to your dog—or to any animal!

5. Focus on walks in the (areea) around your neighborhood until your dog becomes familiar with the territory. Then try some longer trips.

	Spelling Words
1.	poem
2.	idea
3.	create
4.	diary
5.	area
6.	giant
7.	usual
8.	radio
9.	cruel
10.	quiet*
11.	diet
12.	liar
13.	fuel
14.	riot
15.	actual
16.	lion
17.	ruin
18.	trial
19.	rodeo
20.	science

1. create **(1 point)**   4. cruel **(1)**

2. quiet **(1)**   5. area **(1)**

3. fuel **(1)**

Write a Want Ad What qualities make a good dog guide? What natural instincts does a dog guide have to learn to overcome? **On a separate sheet of paper, write a want ad for *Working Dog Weekly* describing the job of dog guide. Use Spelling Words from the list.** Responses will vary. **(5)**

Name _____

The Meaningful Word

**Read the advertisement. Then use each underlined word to complete
the numbered sentences. Be careful! The underlined words have more
than one meaning.**

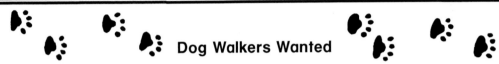

Dog Walkers Wanted

   Helping Hound, the biggest guide dog school in the state,
is looking for young people like you. We need your help to train
our future guide dogs. You can take a dog on a trip to the park
or around the block. You can play with your dog, teach it not to
bark at other dogs, and help break it of other bad habits. You'll
be training your dog to suit a new owner. You'll have fun as you
help your helping hound pass its final exams! Apply today.

1. I covered my ears to <u>block **(1 point)**</u> out the sound of the
   jackhammer.

2. Be careful not to <u>trip **(1)**</u> on that curb.

3. If you <u>hound **(1)**</u> your teacher for less homework, you
   might get more instead!

4. My father bought us tickets for a <u>train **(1)**</u> ride this weekend.

5. If you get tired, take a <u>break **(1)**</u> before you go back to work.

6. Could you please <u>pass **(1)**</u> me the potatoes?

7. Every day, my mother wears a <u>suit **(1)**</u> to work.

8. We drove around looking for a place to <u>park **(1)**</u> the car.

9. Speak into the microphone and <u>state **(1)**</u> your name clearly.

10. The thin white <u>bark **(1)**</u> of the birch tree feels soft, like
    tissue paper.

Assessment Tip: Total **10** Points

Name _____

Commas, Commas, and More Commas!

Commas in a Series A **series** is a list of three or more items. Use commas to separate the items in a series. Put a comma after each item in a series except the last one. Use *and* or *or* before the last item in a series.

I like cats, dogs, rabbits, **and** all kinds of animals.

Add commas to the sentences below that have items in a series. If the sentence does not contain a series, write *none* after the sentence. (1 point for each correct sentence**)**

1. German shepherds, golden retrievers, and other breeds can be trained as dog guides.

2. Dogs and monkeys are trained to help people with disabilities. none

3. Our dogs are named Riley, Maggie, and Midnight.

4. My cousin takes her dog to visit nursing homes, retirement centers, and hospitals.

5. Parakeets, parrots, cockatoos, and mynah birds can learn to talk.

6. In our classroom are fish, turtles, and a snake.

7. Other classrooms have guinea pigs, hamsters, and gerbils.

8. Our calico cat is black, brown, white, and orange.

9. Marla's cat is orange and white. none

10. Tim's cat is black, gray, and white.

Name _____

Yes, I Can

More Uses for Commas Use commas to set off the words *yes*, *no*, and *well* when they appear as introductory words at the beginning of a sentence. Also use a comma or commas to set off the names of people who are addressed directly.

Introductory word:	**Yes,** Mr. Baxter's dog is devoted to him.
Direct address:	**Kristin,** please help Mr. Baxter with the door.
	Would you walk the dog, **Jamie**?
Introductory word	
and direct address:	**Well, Kristin,** that is a good idea.

Add commas where needed in the sentences below.
(1 point for each correct sentence**)**

1. I'm afraid I'm not feeling well today, Jamie.

2. Well, Mr. Baxter, I'll walk Buster for you.

3. Thank you, Jamie.

4. Why isn't Mr. Baxter walking Buster, Kristin?

5. Well, I guess Jamie wants to help him.

6. It's nice of you, Jamie, to help Mr. Baxter.

7. Well, Kristin, Mr. Baxter is a helpful neighbor.

8. Yes, he is, Jamie.

9. Kristin, have you ever walked Buster?

10. No, Myron, I haven't.

Assessment Tip: Total **10** Points

Name _____

I Feed, Groom, and Pet My Cat

Combining Sentences by Creating a Series A good writer puts items in a series in one sentence, instead of mentioning them in separate sentences.

> **Awkward:** Dogs make good pets. Cats make good pets. Birds do too.
> **Revised:** Dogs, cats, and birds make good pets.

Sophie is drafting an essay. Revise the essay by putting items into a series where needed. Write your revision below. (10 points)

> My cat, Buzz, greets me at the door when I come home from school. He greets me when I come home from a friend's house. He greets me when I come home from an appointment. Buzz meows. He purrs. He rubs against my legs. Then I pick him up. Buzz purrs while I tell him about the spelling test. He purrs while I tell him about my friend's cat or events of the day.
>
> I like to take care of Buzz. I feed him. I groom him. I play with him. He can make me feel calm. He can make me feel loved. He can make me feel special. Buzz is like a patient person with fur. He is like a person with long whiskers. He is like a person with a tail.

My cat, Buzz, greets me at the door when I come home from school, a friend's house, or an appointment. Buzz meows, purrs, and rubs against my legs. Then I pick him up. Buzz purrs while I tell him about the spelling test, my friend's cat, or events of the day.

I like to take care of Buzz. I feed him, groom him, and play with him. He can make me feel calm, loved, and special. Buzz is like a patient person with fur, long whiskers, and a tail.

Name _____

Writing Instructions

In *Mom's Best Friend*, Pete Jackson at The Seeing Eye gives Leslie's mother verbal instructions for training her new dog guide, Ursula. **Instructions** tell you how to do or make something. When you are trying to learn a new skill, written instructions are helpful. Good written instructions clearly explain all of the steps to be followed and the order in which the steps are to be done.

Complete the graphic organizer below to help you plan and organize written instructions for doing something you know how to do, such as a dance, a particular sports move, or a game. If possible, do the activity yourself and use the graphic organizer to outline each step.

Instructions for **(1 point)** _____

Materials **(1)** _____

Step 1 **(1)** _____

    Step 2 **(1)** _____

        Step 3 **(1)** _____

    Step 4 **(1)** _____

        Step 5 **(1)** _____

Using the information you recorded, write your instructions on a separate sheet of paper. First, write a title that describes what the instructions are for. Then list any materials that are needed. Explain each step in order, using sequence words such as *first*, *next*, or *last*. Include diagrams or pictures if they help clarify the process. When you finish your instructions, share them with your classmates. (5)

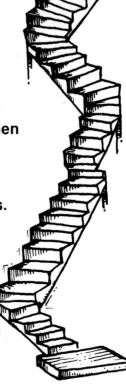

Assessment Tip: Total **12** Points

Combining Sentences by Using Introductory Phrases

Good writers avoid using a string of short, choppy sentences to express their ideas. One way to streamline your writing is to combine two choppy sentences into one sentence with an introductory phrase.

> Mom will walk solo with Ursula. She will do this after ten practice runs with Pete.

> **After ten practice runs with Pete,** Mom will walk solo with Ursula.

Read the instructions for acting as a sighted guide. Then revise them by combining two short sentences into a single sentence with an introductory phrase. Punctuate introductory phrases correctly.
Responses may vary slightly. **(12 points)**

Techniques for Being a Sighted Guide

Touch the person's elbow, forearm, or hand lightly. Do this at the start. Stand still a moment. Let the person grasp your arm just above the elbow. Walk where the person wants to go. Use a comfortable pace. Stay slightly ahead. Guide with your words and body movement. Tell the person what is ahead, such as stairs or a curb. Do this when approaching an obstacle. State whether you will turn right or left. This should be done just before turning. When you reach your destination, the person will release his or her grasp.

Techniques for Being a Sighted Guide

At the start, touch the person's elbow, forearm, or hand lightly. Standing still a

moment, let the person grasp your arm just above the elbow. Using a comfortable

pace, walk where the person wants to go. Staying slightly ahead, guide with your

words and body movement. When approaching an obstacle, tell the person what is

ahead, such as stairs or a curb. Just before turning, state whether you will turn right

or left. When you reach your destination, the person will release his or her grasp.

Name _____

It's a Secret

Write each word from the box in the correct category.

things done in front of an audience

opera **(1 point)** _____

demonstration **(1)** _____

parts of a culture

heritage **(1)** _____

traditions **(1)** _____

describing words

noble **(1)** _____

rhythmic **(1)** _____

action word

impressed **(1)** _____

word for musical support

accompaniment **(1)** _____

Choose two words from the box and write a sentence using both words.

(2) _____

_____

> ### Vocabulary
>
> heritage
> impressed
> traditions
> opera
> accompaniment
> demonstration
> noble
> rhythmic

Assessment Tip: Total **10** Points

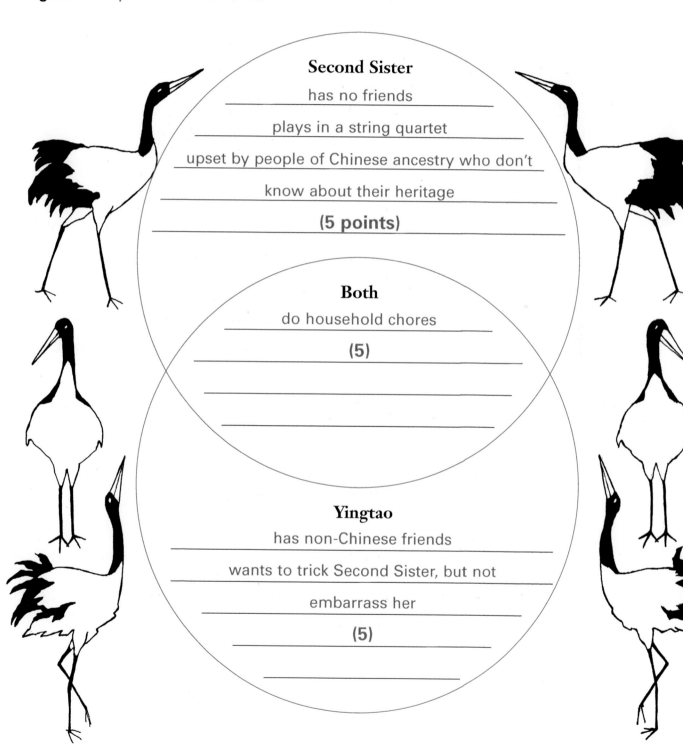

Name _____

Different and Alike

Fill in the diagram to compare and contrast Second Sister and Yingtao. Sample answers shown.

Second Sister

has no friends

plays in a string quartet

upset by people of Chinese ancestry who don't

know about their heritage

(5 points)

Both

do household chores

(5)

Yingtao

has non-Chinese friends

wants to trick Second Sister, but not

embarrass her

(5)

Name _____

Plot the Trick

Complete the story map below to show the main elements of the story.

Characters	Setting
Main Characters: Second Sister, Third Sister, Yingtao, Paul Eng **(1)**	**First Setting:** **Time:** during and after dinner **Place:** the family's home **(1)**
Minor Characters: Father, Mother, Eldest Brother, Kim O'Meara, Mrs. O'Meara, Melanie Eng **(1)**	**Second Setting:** **Time:** during spring vacation **Place:** the Science Center **(1)**

Plot

Problem: Second Sister has made no friends. She is angry at Paul Eng for not knowing as much about Chinese customs and traditions as she thinks he should.

Events:

1. During a family dinner, Second Sister tells about her erhu demonstration and her scorn for Paul Eng's lack of cultural knowledge. **(1)**

2. After dinner, Third Sister and Yingtao let Second Sister overhear them saying that Paul asked if she goes on dates. **(1)**

3. At the Science Center, Third Sister, Yingtao, and Kim let Paul overhear them talking about how Second Sister is impressed by Paul's baseball and math skills. **(1)**

4. Later in the cafeteria, Paul asks if Second Sister goes out on dates. **(1)**

Resolution: Paul and Second Sister think that the other would like to go out on a date. **(2)**

Assessment Tip: Total **10** Points

Similarity Search

Read the passage. Then complete the activity on page 42.

Trevisa's Favorite Teachers

Trevisa had two favorite teachers: Mr. Yetto, her third-grade teacher, and the fifth-grade teacher, Mrs. McIlvaine, who was Trevisa's teacher now.

Mr. Yetto was young and athletic. He had played football in college and still liked sports, just like Trevisa. He was kind and often called on Trevisa to answer questions during class discussions to help her get over her shyness. But Mr. Yetto could also be strict, and he did not accept excuses. If a student didn't turn in his or her homework on time, he marked that student's grade down. On Fridays Mr. Yetto did yo-yo tricks for the class after lunch. He saved new tricks to show them for the weeks when they had worked especially hard.

Unlike Mr. Yetto, Mrs. McIlvaine was older. She did not like sports, but she loved stories and plays. On Fridays she allowed her students to perform skits during class. Once Danny Pine and David Ginsburg performed a skit in which Danny wore a white wig and played the role of Mrs. McIlvaine herself. He imitated her voice and even remembered certain phrases she used. Mrs. McIlvaine laughed and laughed. But like Mr. Yetto, Mrs. McIlvaine could also be strict. Once, when Trevisa tried writing a book report in very tiny handwriting, just to see if she could do it, Mrs. McIlvaine made her rewrite it. "I can't even read this!" she wrote across the page in red ink. But after Trevisa rewrote her report and turned it in again, Mrs. McIlvaine wrote, "I'm glad I can read this now, because it is just marvelous!"

Name _____

Similarity Search continued

**Fill in the Venn diagram below to show some ways Mr. Yetto
and Mrs. McIlvaine are alike and different.**

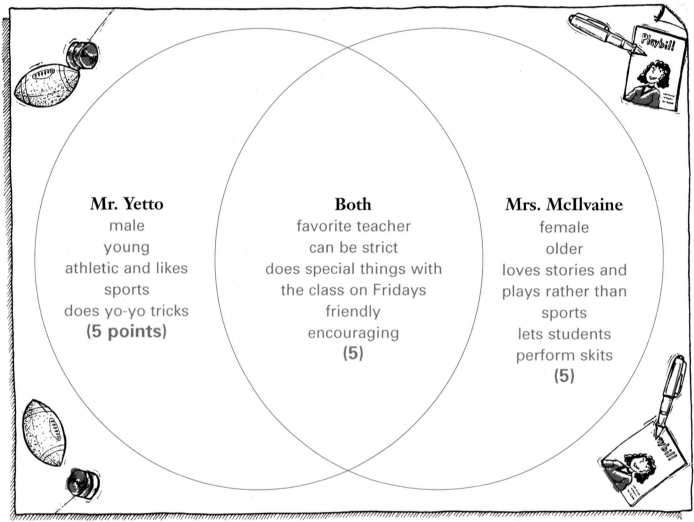

Mr. Yetto
male
young
athletic and likes
sports
does yo-yo tricks
(5 points)

Both
favorite teacher
can be strict
does special things with
the class on Fridays
friendly
encouraging
(5)

Mrs. McIlvaine
female
older
loves stories and
plays rather than
sports
lets students
perform skits
(5)

Now write a paragraph in which you describe how the two teachers are alike.
Sample answer shown. **(5)**

Mr. Yetto and Mrs. McIlvaine are both teachers Trevisa likes a lot. Both are friendly,

kind, and encouraging, but can also be strict. Both plan special events to do with

their class on Fridays.

Assessment Tip: Total **20** Points

Name _____

Tricky Endings

**Read the speech below. Circle the *-ed* and *-ing* endings of the
underlined words. Then write those words on the lines with each *-ing*
ending changed to an *-ed*, and each *-ed* to an *-ing*. Use the new
words to complete the sentences at the bottom of the page.**

It's too bad that Tanya keeps <u>ignoring</u> Raul! He was
<u>admiring</u> how hard she <u>studied</u> for the math test. He's always
<u>dropping</u> by to say, "Do you think she <u>noticed</u> me at the
<u>wrestling</u> match?" **(6 points)**

ignored **(1)** _____

admired **(1)** _____

studying **(1)** _____

dropped **(1)** _____

noticing **(1)** _____

wrestled **(1)** _____

Tanya dropped **(1)** _____ by my locker today. She

didn't know that Raul wrestled **(1)** _____ on the school

team. I told her not to feel bad if he ignored **(1)** _____

her in class. He's too busy studying **(1)** _____ to be

noticing **(1)** _____ anyone! She said she really

admired **(1)** _____ his hard work.

Theme 4: **Person to Person**   43
Assessment Tip: Total **18** Points

Name _____

Words with *-ed* or *-ing*

A **base word** is a word to which endings can be added. When
a base word ends with *e*, you usually drop the *e* when *-ed* or *-ing*
is added. If a base word does not end with *e*, you usually add
the ending *-ed* or *-ing* without a spelling change.

amuse + ing = amus**ing**   direct + ing = direct**ing**

When a one-syllable word ends with a vowel and a consonant,
you usually double the consonant when adding *-ed* or *-ing*.
When a two-syllable word ends with a vowel and a consonant,
you often do not double the consonant when adding *-ed* or *-ing*.

plan + ed = plan**ned**   cover + ed = cover**ed**

► The spelling of *mixed* differs from the usual spelling pattern.
Although *mix* is a one-syllable word, the final consonant is
not doubled when *-ed* is added.

**Write each Spelling Word under the heading that shows
what happens to the base word when *-ed* or *-ing* is added.**
Order of answers for each category may vary.

Spelling Words

1. covered
2. directing
3. bragging
4. amusing
5. offered
6. planned
7. rising
8. deserved
9. visiting
10. mixed*
11. swimming
12. sheltered
13. resulting
14. spotted
15. suffering
16. arrested
17. squeezing
18. ordered
19. decided
20. hitting

Final *e* Dropped

amusing (**1 point**)

rising (**1**)

deserved (**1**)

squeezing (**1**)

decided (**1**)

Final Consonant Doubled

bragging (**1**)

planned (**1**)

swimming (**1**)

spotted (**1**)

hitting (**1**)

No Spelling Change

covered (**1**)

directing (**1**)

offered (**1**)

visiting (**1**)

mixed (**1**)

sheltered (**1**)

resulting (**1**)

suffering (**1**)

arrested (**1**)

ordered (**1**)

Assessment Tip: Total **20** Points

Name _____

Spelling Spree

Ending Clues **Write the Spelling Word that fits each clue.**

1. What *-ing* word is causing others to smile?
2. What *-ed* word was arranged ahead of time?
3. What *-ing* word is moving through water?
4. What *-ed* word was all stirred up?
5. What *-ing* word is pressing hard on something?
6. What *-ing* word is coming about as a consequence?
7. What *-ed* word was commanded?
8. What *-ing* word is striking?

1. amusing **(1 point)**
2. planned **(1)**
3. swimming **(1)**
4. mixed **(1)**

5. squeezing **(1)**
6. resulting **(1)**
7. ordered **(1)**
8. hitting **(1)**

Finding Words **Each word below is hidden in a Spelling Word. Write the Spelling Word.**

9. serve — deserved **(1)**
10. rest — arrested **(1)**
11. over — covered **(1)**
12. off — offered **(1)**
13. pot — spotted **(1)**
14. rag — bragging **(1)**
15. she — sheltered **(1)**

Spelling Words

1. covered
2. directing
3. bragging
4. amusing
5. offered
6. planned
7. rising
8. deserved
9. visiting
10. mixed*
11. swimming
12. sheltered
13. resulting
14. spotted
15. suffering
16. arrested
17. squeezing
18. ordered
19. decided
20. hitting

Assessment Tip: Total **15** Points

Proofreading and Writing

Name _____

Circle the five misspelled Spelling Words in this diary entry that Yinglan might have written. Then write each word correctly.

Dear Diary,

Well, I'm still suffring from shyness around Paul Eng. Today I spotted him in the hall, visitting with some other students. Although nervous, I desided to go say hello. I was only a few steps away when Paul saw me. Suddenly, I felt all my blood riseing to my face. I ended up direckting my eyes straight at the floor and walking right past Paul. Why on earth am I so afraid of him?

Spelling Words

1. covered
2. directing
3. bragging
4. amusing
5. offered
6. planned
7. rising
8. deserved
9. visiting
10. mixed*
11. swimming
12. sheltered
13. resulting
14. spotted
15. suffering
16. arrested
17. squeezing
18. ordered
19. decided
20. hitting

1. suffering **(1 point)**
2. visiting **(1)**
3. decided **(1)**
4. rising **(1)**
5. directing **(1)**

✏ **Write a Description** Have you ever wanted to have a secret admirer? What would that person look like? What qualities would he or she have? What interests would you have in common?

On a separate sheet of paper, write a description of your ideal secret admirer. Use Spelling Words from the list. Responses will vary. **(5)**

Assessment Tip: Total **10** Points

Name _____

Pinpointing Prefixes

Read the dictionary entries. Then in the sentences below, underline the word with a prefix. Write the definition of the word after the sentence.

> *in-* or *im-* A prefix that means "not."
>
> *re-* A prefix that means "again" or "back."
>
> *un-* A prefix that means "not."

1. After waiting so long, the people were <u>impatient</u> for the play to begin. **(1)**
   restless; not patient **(2)**

2. My uncle likes to <u>refresh</u> himself with a nap before going out to dinner. **(1)** to make fresh again **(2)**

3. Nina thought it was <u>unfair</u> to have a science test the morning after the school concert. **(1)** not fair **(2)**

4. I wrote down the <u>incorrect</u> directions and got lost. **(1)**
   not correct; wrong **(2)**

5. The mayor used words we didn't understand, so we asked her to <u>rephrase</u> what she said. **(1)** to phrase again; restate **(2)**

6. When she feels <u>unhappy</u>, Brenda cheers herself up by playing soccer with her friends. **(1)** sad **(2)**

7. Jesse's visits to the doctor are <u>infrequent</u>, because he rarely gets sick. **(1)** not frequent **(2)**

8. When I'm in the city, I like to <u>revisit</u> my old neighborhood. **(1)** to visit again **(2)**

Assessment Tip: Total **24** Points

Name _____

Hey! Let's Play!

Interjections An *interjection* is a word or words that express strong feeling.
An interjection usually appears at the beginning of a sentence.
It can be followed by either a comma or an exclamation point, depending
on how strong a feeling is expressed.

> **Common Interjections**
>
> Well   Wow   Hey   Ouch   Whew   Oh, no   Oh

**Write an interjection and appropriate punctuation on each blank
line below.** Answers will vary.

1. Hey! **(1 point)** _____ Where is the music for our rehearsal?

2. Oh, **(1)** _____ here it is.

3. Well, **(1)** _____ let's start with the piece by Brubeck.

4. Wow! **(1)** _____ I have a long trumpet solo!

5. Whew! **(1)** _____ I made it all the way through without any big errors.

6. Ah, **(1)** _____ that was beautiful.

7. Ouch, **(1)** _____ I stubbed my toe on this chair.

8. Oh, no, **(1)** _____ we're going to practice the hardest part.

9. Well, **(1)** _____ let's get started.

10. Wow! **(1)** _____ We're good!

Assessment Tip: Total **10** Points

Name _____

"What Kind of Music Do You Like?" I Asked

Quotations A *direct quotation* gives a speaker's exact words. Set off exact words with quotation marks. Begin each quotation with a capital letter. Place end punctuation inside quotation marks. Use commas to separate most quotations from the rest of the sentence. If a quotation is two sentences, use a period after the speaker's name.

> Clara said, "I like to listen to all kinds of music."
>
> "Yesterday," she said, "I heard a recording of Chinese opera."
>
> "I liked it," said Clara. "Where can I see a performance?"

Rewrite each quotation below, adding needed punctuation marks and capital letters.

1. Sara asked what did the music of ancient Greece sound like

   Sara asked, "What did the music of ancient Greece sound like?" **(2 points)**

   _____

2. nobody really knows said Ms. Walter.

   "Nobody really knows," said Ms. Walter. **(2)**

3. Lacey said I like the new music from African musicians.

   Lacey said, "I like the new music from African musicians." **(2)**

   _____

4. Lacey, Ms. Walter asked, where can I hear new music from Africa?

   "Lacey," Ms. Walter asked, "where can I hear new music from Africa?" **(2)**

   _____

5. you can hear it on the radio said Lacey it's on a program called
   World Music Today

   "You can hear it on the radio," said Lacey. "It's on a program called

   World Music Today." **(2)**

Name _____

Grandma said, "Yes."

Punctuating Quotations A good writer is careful to punctuate sentences correctly. An incorrectly punctuated sentence is easily misunderstood.

Incorrect: Mrs. Voss said Ana please help me.

Corrected: "Mrs. Voss," said Ana. "Please help me."

Corrected: Mrs. Voss said, "Ana, please help me."

Megan is writing about a visit with her grandmother. She has included exactly what she said and exactly what her grandmother said. Proofread Megan's dialogue, correcting any mistakes in punctuating quotations. (1 point each)

"Your great-grandfather was born in Ireland, Nana said.

I said Wow, I never knew that!"

His parents Nana said owned a small store where all the family

worked.

"Didn't my great-grandfather want to work in the store" I asked.

There were, Nana explained already two older sisters working in the

store, and there would not be enough work for him.

I asked "What did he do?

He had read so much about America that he decided he wanted to

see it for himself," Nana said The next time you visit, I'll tell you about

his first job in New York City."

Assessment Tip: Total **20** Points

Name _____

Writing a How-To Paragraph

When you want to tell readers how to do something, write a
how-to paragraph.

**Use this page to plan and organize a how-to paragraph. First,
choose a topic like how to wash dishes, how to make a pizza, or how
to tie a certain knot. Next, list the materials that are needed. Then
outline each step, giving details that readers need to know to do
each one. Doing the activity yourself will help you outline each step.**

How to __(1 point)_____

Materials __(1)_____

Step 1 __(2)_____

_____

Step 2 __(2)_____

_____

Step 3 __(2)_____

_____

Step 4 __(2)_____

_____

Step 5 __(2)_____

_____

**Using the information you recorded, write your how-to paragraph on
a separate sheet of paper. In the first sentence, describe what skill
will be taught. Then tell what materials are needed. Next, explain
each step clearly and in order. Use sequence words such as *before,
after,* and *now* to clarify the order. If necessary, include diagrams or
pictures to help readers picture the process. When you finish, work
with your classmates to create a class How-To-Do-It book. (8)**

Name _____

Using Order Words

A careful writer uses **order words** such as *first*, *next*, and *finally* in a how-to paragraph. Order words help readers understand a process and keep track of the sequence of steps.

Read the following how-to paragraph. Then rewrite the paragraph on the lines, adding order words and phrases from the list to make the sequence of steps clearer and to help readers follow the process. Be sure to use correct capitalization and punctuation when you add order words and phrases or combine two sentences.
(12 points)

To clean chopsticks, you will need a big pan, hot water, and dishwashing liquid. Fill the pan with hot water. Add about a teaspoon of dishwashing liquid. Drop the dirty chopsticks in the hot, soapy water. Grab a handful of chopsticks and roll them together like a stack of pencils between your two hands. You hear a burrrr sound. This means the chopsticks are getting really clean! Rinse the chopsticks with clean water.

Order Words

until

next

then

finally

first

now

To clean chopsticks, you will need a big pan, hot water, and dishwashing liquid.

First, fill the pan with hot water. **Next,** add about a teaspoon of dishwashing liquid.

Then drop the dirty chopsticks in the hot, soapy water. **Now** grab a handful of

chopsticks and roll them like a stack of pencils between your two hands **until** you

hear a burrrr sound. This means the chopsticks are getting really clean! **Finally,**

rinse the chopsticks with clean water.

Assessment Tip: Total **12** Points

Name _____

A Writer's Words

Write each word from the box beside the phrase that describes it.

1. very wonderful <u>splendid</u> **(1 point)**

2. writing that is not poetry <u>prose</u> **(1)**

3. a person who invades the privacy of others
   <u>snoop</u> **(1)**

4. a book not to be read by others without permission
   <u>diary</u> **(1)**

5. how you feel when you're not able to do something you've
   been wanting to do <u>disappointed</u> **(1)**

6. a thing that happens to you <u>experience</u> **(1)**

7. what you have done when you have given an article to a newspaper
   for publication <u>submitted</u> **(1)**

8. the opposite of *accepted* <u>rejected</u> **(1)**

9. knowing why things are the way they are <u>understanding</u> **(1)**

Now write three sentences about being a writer. Use at least one vocabulary word in each sentence.

(3) _____

_____

_____

_____

_____

Name _____

Reading Between the Lines

Read the prompt in the first column. Use evidence from the story and your own experiences to make inferences about Leigh.

Answers will vary. Samples are shown.

	Evidence from the Story	Own Experiences	Inferences
• **What kind of person is Leigh?**	When the librarian tells him he still has time to enter a contest to meet a famous author, which he wants to do, he gets right to work. **(2 points)**	Someone who is willing to start a difficult task right away in order to achieve something is industrious. **(2)**	Leigh is industrious. **(2)**
• **How does Leigh feel about his house?**	He says he wasn't sure his friend would like coming to his house because it is small. **(2)**	People who worry that someone else won't like their house may feel ashamed of it, or they may just be worried that the other person will find some reason not to like them. **(2)**	Leigh might feel a little ashamed of his house, or he might just be worried that Barry might stop being his friend. **(2)**

Assessment Tip: Total **12** Points

Name _____

The "Write" Connection

What relationship did each person have with Leigh in *Dear Mr. Henshaw*? Answer in complete sentences.

Miss Neely She convinced Leigh to enter the writing contest. She handed out copies of the Yearbook, which had Leigh's description in it. She invited Leigh to meet Angela Badger after the first prize winner was disqualified. **(2 points)**

Leigh's dad He talked to Leigh on the phone. Leigh wrote about a time he took Leigh on a hauling job. Leigh worried about him getting married. **(2)**

Barry He came to Leigh's house for dinner and had a good time. Leigh was glad Barry was his friend. **(2)**

Leigh's mom She made a great dinner for Leigh and Barry. She and Leigh had a difficult discussion about Leigh's dad. She said she was proud of Leigh when he told her that Angela Badger had called him an author. **(2)**

Angela Badger She read and praised Leigh's description. She gave him advice and told him he was an author, which made him proud. **(2)**

Name _____

Connecting Clues

Read the diary entries that might have been written by Julia.
Then complete the activity on page 57.

Monday, October 1

    Today was my first day at George Washington Elementary School. My old school's name was better: Woodside. I miss the stretch of woods nearby where my best friend Laura and I would go to skip stones in the creek and look for frogs. The area around this school is made out of concrete, even the playground. I sat by myself at lunch.

Tuesday, October 2

    Today my teacher, Mrs. Langley, asked me to stand up in front of the class and tell one exciting fact about where I moved from. My face felt like it was on fire. I said I was from Illinois and on the license plate it says "Land of Lincoln." I thought I saw Mrs. Langley hide a laugh behind her sleeve, but I can't be sure. After that, I was glad I have a desk in the back of the room. When I got home, Mom asked me how school was. I gave her the same answer I'd given the day before, "Okay."

Thursday, October 4

    Today at lunch they had chocolate pudding. I took two because chocolate pudding is my favorite. I was sitting alone (again) reading a book (again) when I heard someone say, "Julia?" It was Megan, the girl with the loud laugh, asking me to sit with her. Megan also had two servings of chocolate pudding. She told a story about her older brother that was so funny I almost choked on my broccoli. Today when Mom asked me how school was, I said, "Pretty good."

Tuesday, October 9

    Today after school Megan and I took her puppy to the park. She showed me how to do a cartwheel in the grass. When Mom asked me how my day was, I said, "Fun." She looked happy.

Name _____

Connecting Clues continued

**Answer each question about the passage on page 56. Below your
answer, write the clues and what you know from your own experience
that helped make the inference.** Sample answers shown.

1. How does Julia feel after the first day at her new school?
   Julia is unhappy after the first day. **(2 points)**

Story Clues		My Own Experience
She says she likes her old school's name better. She thinks the new school is not as attractive. She sits alone at lunch. **(2)**	**+**	It can be scary to start a new school. I might miss my friends and feel lonely without someone to sit with. I also like a grass playground better than a concrete one. **(2)**

2. How does Julia feel about talking in front of the class?
   She is nervous and embarrassed. **(2)**

Story Clues		My Own Experience
Her face turns red. She is glad her desk is in the back. **(2)**	**+**	I know people blush when they are embarrassed. Some people sit in the back of the class so they won't be noticed. **(2)**

3. How do Julia's feelings change after the first week of school?
   She starts to like her new school better after the first week. **(2)**

Story Clues		My Own Experience
At first she tells her Mom school is "okay," but by the second week she says it is "fun." She starts to do things with Megan. **(2)**	**+**	I know that people describe things differently as their feelings change. And I know that having a friend makes school more fun. **(2)**

Name _____

Thanks with Suffixes

Read this letter that Leigh might have written. In the underlined words, circle the suffixes *-ly*, *-ness*, *-ment*, *-ful*, and *-less*. (10 points)

April 3

Dear Mrs. Badger,

    I couldn't believe it when I heard the announce(ment) that I could go to the writers' lunch today. It was wonder(ful) to meet you. Before today, I felt hope(less) about my fit(ness) to be a writer. I was doubt(ful) what I should write. My ideas most(ly) went nowhere. But you gave me encourage(ment) Now I feel fear(less) when I write. I think I'll be in the writing busi(ness) for a long time.

                           Sincere(ly) yours,
                           Leigh Botts

Now, write each word with a suffix beside its correct definition.

1. mostly **(1)** _____ : for the most part
2. hopeless **(1)** _____ : without hope
3. business **(1)** _____ : profession
4. sincerely **(1)** _____ : truly; honestly
5. announcement **(1)** _____ : message
6. wonderful **(1)** _____ : great
7. encouragement **(1)** _____ : a lift in confidence
8. fearless **(1)** _____ : without fear
9. fitness **(1)** _____ : suitability
10. doubtful **(1)** _____ : full of doubts

58   Theme 4: **Person to Person**
Assessment Tip: Total **20** Points

Words with Suffixes (-ly, -ness, -ment, -ful, -less)

A **suffix** is a word part added to the end of a base word. A suffix adds meaning to the word. The word parts -*ly*, -*ness*, -*ment*, -*ful* and -*less* are suffixes. The spelling of the base word is usually not changed when the suffix begins with a consonant.

safe + ly = safe**ly**   cheer + ful = cheer**ful**

pale + ness = pale**ness**   speech + less = speech**less**

enjoy + ment = enjoy**ment**

Order of answers for each category may vary.

Write each Spelling Word under its suffix.

-*ness* or -*ment*	-*ful* or -*less*
enjoyment **(1 point)**	dreadful **(1)**
paleness **(1)**	watchful **(1)**
government **(1)**	speechless **(1)**
closeness **(1)**	breathless **(1)**
goodness **(1)**	cheerful **(1)**
retirement **(1)**	forgetful **(1)**
basement **(1)**	delightful **(1)**
softness **(1)**	countless **(1)**
settlement **(1)**	

-*ly*		
safely **(1)**	actively **(1)**	lately **(1)**

Spelling Words

1. dreadful
2. enjoyment
3. safely
4. watchful
5. speechless
6. paleness
7. breathless
8. government
9. cheerful
10. actively
11. closeness
12. lately
13. goodness
14. retirement
15. forgetful
16. basement
17. softness
18. delightful
19. settlement
20. countless

Theme 4: **Person to Person**   59
Assessment Tip: Total **20** Points

Name _____

Spelling Spree

Adding Suffixes Write the Spelling Word that contains each base word below.

1. soft   softness

2. retire   retirement

3. good   goodness

4. forget   forgetful

5. govern   government

6. breath   breathless

7. settle   settlement

Contrast Clues The second part of each clue contrasts with the first part. Write a Spelling Word for each clue.

Example: not weak, but *powerful*

8. not long ago, but   lately

9. not talkative, but   speechless

10. not careless, but   watchful

11. not distance, but   closeness

12. not grouchy, but   cheerful

13. not wonderful, but   dreadful

14. not darkness, but   paleness

15. not few, but   countless

Spelling Words

1. dreadful
2. enjoyment
3. safely
4. watchful
5. speechless
6. paleness
7. breathless
8. government
9. cheerful
10. actively
11. closeness
12. lately
13. goodness
14. retirement
15. forgetful
16. basement
17. softness
18. delightful
19. settlement
20. countless

Assessment Tip: Total **15** Points

Name _____

Proofreading and Writing

Proofreading Circle the five misspelled Spelling Words in the following newspaper article. Then write each word correctly.

> ### Young Writers Meet Famous Author
>
> The winners of the Young Writers' Yearbook contest had a (delightfull) lunch with Mrs. Angela Badger last week. Some students were speechless upon meeting the popular author, but others (acttively) sought her attention and talked easily with her. Mrs. Badger was impressed by the number of our students who read and write for their own (injoyment). Everyone had a wonderful time, and our young writers returned (safly) to the school. If any students have not yet read the winning stories, copies of the yearbook are available in the supply room in the school (basment.)

1. delightful **(1 point)**
2. actively **(1)**
3. enjoyment **(1)**
4. safely **(1)**
5. basement **(1)**

Spelling Words

1. dreadful
2. enjoyment
3. safely
4. watchful
5. speechless
6. paleness
7. breathless
8. government
9. cheerful
10. actively
11. closeness
12. lately
13. goodness
14. retirement
15. forgetful
16. basement
17. softness
18. delightful
19. settlement
20. countless

Write an Opinion Leigh was disappointed because his story received an honorable mention instead of a prize. In the end, though, it was his story that Mrs. Badger remembered. If you were in Leigh's position, would you rather have won the contest or received Mrs. Badger's praise?

On a separate piece of paper, write a paragraph describing how you would have felt if you were in Leigh's place and why. Use Spelling Words from the list. Responses will vary. **(5)**

Name _____

That's Good or Bad?

A script for *Dear Mr. Henshaw* might contain a scene in which Leigh tells his mother about meeting Angela Badger. Rewrite each sentence by first replacing the underlined word with a positive connotation. Then, write the sentence again replacing the word with a negative connotation. Choose your words from the list below.

odd	aroma	chatted	notorious
famous	inventive	stink	jabbered

1. "Mom, Mrs. Badger called my story original!"

   "Mom, Mrs. Badger called my story inventive!" **(2 points)**

   "Mom, Mrs. Badger called my story odd!" **(2)**

2. "She liked what I wrote about the smell of grapes in the sun."

   "She liked what I wrote about the aroma of grapes in the sun." **(2)**

   "She liked what I wrote about the stink of grapes in the sun." **(2)**

3. "We asked her what it felt like to be a well-known author."

   "We asked her what it felt like to be a famous author." **(2)**

   "We asked her what it felt like to be a notorious author." **(2)**

4. "The other kids talked with Mrs. Badger more than I did."

   "The other kids chatted with Mrs. Badger more than I did." **(2)**

   "The other kids jabbered with Mrs. Badger more than I did." **(2)**

Assessment Tip: Total **16** Points

Name _____

Make It Shorter!

Abbreviations An **abbreviation** is a shortened form of a word. Most abbreviations begin with a capital letter and end with a period. Most abbreviations should only be used in special kinds of writing, such as in addresses and lists.

Common Abbreviations					
Mr.	Mister	St.	Street	Co.	Company
Mrs.	married woman	Ave.	Avenue	Inc.	Incorporated
Ms.	any woman	Apt.	apartment	WV	West Virginia
Dr.	Doctor	P. O.	Post Office	TX	Texas
Jr.	Junior	Dec.	December	CA	California
Sr.	Senior	Mon.	Monday	ME	Maine

Rewrite each group of words using abbreviations where possible.

1. Morgan Glass, Incorporated   Morgan Glass, Inc. **(1 point)**

2. Mister David Kowalsky, Junior   Mr. David Kowalsky, Jr. **(1)**

3. Wednesday, February 28, 2004   Wed., Feb. 28, 2004 **(1)**

4. 2557 Hastings Avenue, Apartment 4   2557 Hastings Ave., Apt. 4 **(1)**

5. Bangor, Maine   Bangor, ME **(1)**

6. Post Office Box 1287   P. O. Box 1287 **(1)**

7. Star, West Virginia   Star, WV **(1)**

8. 25 Westgate Road, Apartment 6

    25 Westgate Rd. Apt. 6 **(1)**

Name _____

Titles, "Titles," and More Titles

Titles Capitalize the first, the last, and each important word in the titles of books, movies, or newspapers. Capitalize forms of the word *be*, including *is, are,* and *am*. Capitalize words like *and, in, of, to, a,* and *the* only when they are the first or last word in a title. Put titles in italic type or underline them. Titles of short works, such as short stories, poems, articles, songs, and chapters of books are enclosed in quotation marks.

Newspaper: My mother reads <u>The Wall Street Journal</u> every day.

Book: I read <u>Make Way for Ducklings</u> to my younger brother.

Chapter: The first chapter of this book is called "On the Beach."

Each of the sentences below contains a title. Rewrite each title correctly.

1. The book The cat in the hat was a childhood favorite of mine.
   <u>The Cat in the Hat</u> **(2 points)**

2. Lester read a book called the second floor mystery.
   <u>The Second Floor Mystery</u> **(2)**

3. The disappearance of the ladder is the name of the first chapter.
   "The Disappearance of the Ladder" **(2)**

4. Chris saw the old movie My friend flicka.
   <u>My Friend Flicka</u> **(2)**

5. Have you seen the review in The gladeview gazette, our school paper?
   <u>The Gladeview Gazette</u> **(2)**

6. Do you know the words to the song America?
   "America" **(2)**

7. Deer at dusk is one of my favorite poems
   "Deer at Dusk" **(2)**

Name _____

Using Abbreviations

A good writer uses abbreviations only in special kinds of writing, such as lists and addresses. Marcus used abbreviations where he should have written out the entire word, and wrote out words that should be abbreviated.

Rewrite and correct the address. Then proofread the body of the letter. Correct each error above the line. (1 point for each correct response.)

Marcus Chester, Junior _Marcus Chester, Jr._____

218 Mulberry Street _218 Mulberry St._____

Bowen, California _Bowen, CA_____

             Mr.
Dear MisterVasquez:

                                       Saturday
    I am a big fan of your work. Last Sat. I read your latest mystery. It was
                                              road
exciting. When Randolph and Kildare chased Brad and Chris down the rd.,

I read as fast as I could to find out what would happen next.
                             North Carolina
    Have you ever thought of setting a story in NC? If you came here to
                              apartment
do research, I could help you. My family lives in an apt. in Charlotte, and we
                        street
would be happy to have you stay with us. Our st. has a big, dark old house
                                      August
you would like. My friends and I saw something mysterious there last Aug.

    Thanks for writing such great books.

                             Your fan,

                             Marcus

                             Marcus Chester

Name _____

Writing a Journal Entry

Leigh Botts, the main character in *Dear Mr. Henshaw*, keeps a journal. A **journal** is a notebook, diary, folder, or file in which you can keep a record of your thoughts, ideas, and experiences.

On the lines below, write a journal entry about a day in your own life. Follow these guidelines:

▶ **Write the date at the beginning. You might also want to include the location.**

▶ **Write in the first person, using the pronouns *I, me, my, mine, we,* and *our*.**

▶ **Narrate or describe the day's events or experiences.**

▶ **Include personal thoughts, feelings, reactions, questions, and ideas.**

▶ **Use details to describe what you saw or experienced.**

(10 points)

_____

_____

_____

_____

_____

_____

_____

_____

_____

When you finish your journal entry, you may want to share it with a friend or a classmate.

Assessment Tip: Total **10** Points

Expanding Sentences with Adjectives

An **adjective** like *plump* or *icy* describes a noun or pronoun. Good writers use adjectives to create a clear, vivid picture of what they are describing or narrating.

Read this journal entry that Leigh Botts might have written after a day of hiking. Then rewrite it on the lines, adding adjectives from the list to bring Leigh's description to life. Use as many adjectives as you can, joining related adjectives with *and* or a comma if appropriate.

Saturday, March 10
Today I took a hike through the woods. A cloud of monarch butterflies fluttered through the air. As I leaned quietly against the bark of a tree trunk, they landed in the leaves above. Soon the afternoon sun appeared like a coin against the hills. I knew it was time to go home for supper, but the gas station is so noisy compared with the silence of the forest.

Adjectives

dark	lonely
distant	orange
huge	green
delicate	short
scratchy	busy
golden	cool
crowded	small
shiny	

Responses may vary. **(15 points)**

Today I took a **short** hike through the **lonely** woods. A **small** cloud of

monarch butterflies, **orange** and **delicate,** fluttered through the **cool** air.

As I leaned quietly against the **scratchy** bark of a tree trunk, they landed

in the **green** leaves above. Soon the afternoon sun, **golden** and **shiny,**

appeared like a **huge** coin against the **dark, distant** hills. I knew it was

time to go home for supper, but the gas station, **busy** and **crowded,** is so

noisy compared with the silence of the forest.

Name _____

Vocabulary Surfing

Read this newspaper article about a new surfing school. Complete the article by filling in each blank with the correct word from the list.

Surf's Up!

by Pedro Hernandez

> ### Vocabulary
> chauffeur
> surfing
> maneuvering
> surfaced
> taunted

Los Angeles, CA—When I heard about Sammy's Wave Rider Shack, a new __surfing **(2 points)**__ school, I just had to take a lesson. Since my mom's car was in the shop, I asked my uncle to __chauffeur **(2)**__ me to the beach.

I had never taken a surfing lesson in my life. I was afraid of being __taunted **(2)**__ by the more experienced surfers! I was surprised to find that everyone was friendly. My surfing teacher was named Jillian, and she was very patient. We paddled out into the ocean and waited for some waves. Jillian taught me what to do when a wave came.

When the first wave came, I tried to stand on my surfboard. Unfortunately, I got knocked off the board and into the ocean. When I __surfaced **(2)**__, Jillian was smiling. "Way to go!" she said. "That's great for a first try."

After an hour in the water, I was __maneuvering **(2)**__ my way around pretty well. I was certainly no expert, but I was beginning to enjoy myself. I'll definitely go back to Sammy's for another lesson.

Assessment Tip: Total **10** Points

Relationship Diagram

In the Venn diagram, compare and contrast the relationship between Hector and Mando in *Summer on Wheels* and the Wright brothers in *The Wright Brothers: How They Invented the Airplane.* List two things in each part of the diagram.
Answers will vary. Sample answers are shown.

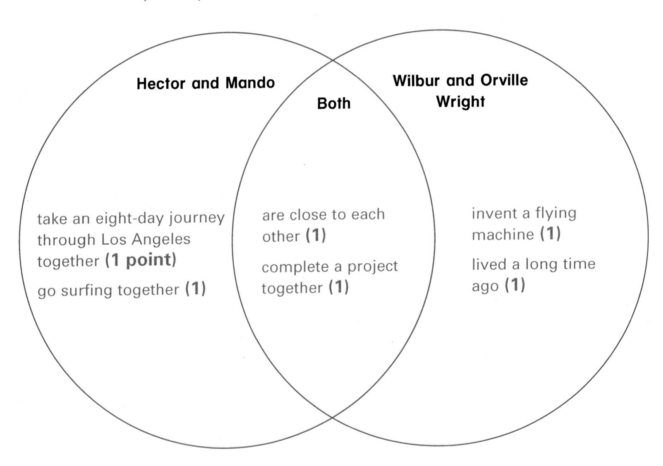

Hector and Mando

Both

Wilbur and Orville Wright

take an eight-day journey through Los Angeles together **(1 point)**

go surfing together **(1)**

are close to each other **(1)**

complete a project together **(1)**

invent a flying machine **(1)**

lived a long time ago **(1)**

Based on your diagram, what would you say are the biggest similarities between the relationships in these two stories? Answers will vary, but should reflect the contents of the Venn diagram. **(2 points)**

_____

_____

_____

_____

Assessment Tip: Total **8** Points

Name _____

Storyteller's Craft

Compare Gary Soto's storytelling method in *Summer on Wheels* with
Beverly Cleary's method in *Dear Mr. Henshaw*. Write your thoughts
and ideas in the chart. Wording of answers will vary.

	Summer on Wheels	Dear Mr. Henshaw
How does the author tell the story?	as a narrative told by an outside observer **(1 point)**	through journal entries and letters written by a story character **(1)**
Whose point of view is the story told from?	the narrator's **(1)**	the main character's **(1)**
How do readers know what the main character is thinking?	The narrator tells us; we use clues in the character's actions and words. **(1)**	Leigh tells us how he is feeling. **(1)**
What do you like or dislike about this way of telling a story?	Answers will vary. **(1)**	Answers will vary. **(1)**

Theme 4: **Person to Person**   71

Assessment Tip: Total **8** Points

Name _____

The "Wright" Match

Write the letter to match each word with its definition.

d **(1 point)** ___ buffeted   a. uneven and unpredictable

b **(1)** _____ elated   b. very, very happy

e **(1)** _____ clattered   c. not a good sign

c **(1)** _____ unfavorable   d. knocked around

a **(1)** _____ erratic   e. moved with a loud, rattling noise

Fill in each blank with one of the Key Vocabulary words from the above activity.

1. "The weather conditions are ___unfavorable **(1)**___ for a flight today," the pilot said with a frown.

2. The mechanic's tools ___clattered **(1)**___ to the ground when he knocked them over.

3. The plane was ___buffeted **(1)**___ by strong gusts of wind, and the passengers were nervous.

4. The plane's flight was short and ___erratic **(1)**___ because of the violent wind.

5. When the plane finally landed, the passengers were so ___elated **(1)**___ that they cheered!

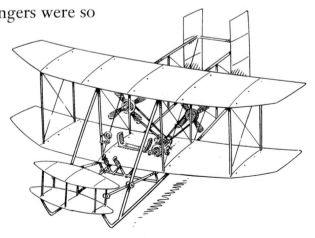

Assessment Tip: Total **10** Points

Name _____

Test Practice

Use the three steps you've learned to choose the best answer for these multiple-choice vocabulary questions about *The Wright Brothers*. Fill in the circle for the best answer in the answer rows at the bottom of the page.

1. Which word means about the same as *shudder* on page 438I?

    A break

    B rise

    C hurry

    D tremble

2. The author writes, "Then Wilbur loosened the restraining rope that held the Flyer in place." Which word means about the same as *restraining*?

    F lowering

    G holding

    H untying

    J hoisting

3. Read this sentence from the story. "They woke up that morning to freezing temperatures and a blustery 27-mile-an-hour wind." What does *blustery* mean?

    A blowing hard and noisily

    B bringing rain

    C causing snow and ice

    D making a whispery sound

4. Read these sentences from the story. "The conditions were very unfavorable," wrote Wilbur. "Nevertheless, as we had set our minds on being home by Christmas, we determined to go ahead." What does *unfavorable* mean?

    F likely to change

    G likely to be the same

    H likely to cause success

    J likely to cause problems

ANSWER ROWS   I Ⓐ Ⓑ Ⓒ **Ⓓ** (5 points)   3 **Ⓐ** Ⓑ Ⓒ Ⓓ (5)

2 Ⓕ **Ⓖ** Ⓗ Ⓙ (5)   4 Ⓕ Ⓖ Ⓗ **Ⓙ** (5)

Continue on page 74.

Name _____

Test Practice continued

5. Which word means the opposite of *hoisted* on page 438J?

   A folded

   B raised

   C lighted

   D dropped

6. The author writes, "They had to go inside frequently to warm their hands by the carbide-can stove." Which word means the opposite of *frequently*?

   F often

   G quickly

   H rarely

   J soon

7. In paragraph 1 on page 438K, what does the word *site* mean?

   A the place where something happens

   B something that is seen

   C a sandy place such as a beach

   D a platform for launching a plane

8. Read these sentences from the story. "A boy could have thrown a ball as far as the Flyer had flown. But the Wright brothers were elated." What does the word *elated* probably mean?

   F curious

   G eager

   H joyful

   J disappointed

ANSWER ROWS   5 Ⓐ Ⓑ Ⓒ **Ⓓ** (5 points)   7 **Ⓐ** Ⓑ Ⓒ Ⓓ (5)
              6 Ⓕ Ⓖ **Ⓗ** Ⓙ (5)   8 Ⓕ Ⓖ **Ⓗ** Ⓙ (5)

Assessment Tip: Total **40** Points

Name _____

Was It a Good Decision?

Read the paragraphs. Then answer the questions.

A big wave rose up and both Martha and Lily caught it. As they surfed toward the beach, Martha cut gracefully across the curl of the wave.

This was Lily's first time on a surfboard. As soon as the wave broke, she tumbled head over heels. Just as she popped out of the water, she was hit by another big wave. On the next wave, she managed to keep herself above water.

Pausing to catch her breath, Lily saw Martha heading back out to deeper water. "Let's go!" Martha said. "These are big waves."

"Maybe a little too big," thought Lily, but she didn't want Martha to think she was scared. With great effort, Lily climbed back on her board and headed out.

Sample answers shown.

1. Lily has two problems. What are they? She is just a beginner and the waves are too big for her. **(2 points)** She is worried that Martha will think she is scared if she stops surfing. **(2)**

2. What is her solution to her problems? Lily decides to continue surfing to show her friend that she is not scared. **(2)**

3. Do you think Lily's decision is wise? Why or why not? No. Her decision is not good because surfing is a dangerous sport and she could get hurt. **(2)**

4. What other solutions might Lily have tried? She could decided not to go back out. She could have looked for a place with smaller waves. She could have asked Martha for help finding a place with smaller waves. **(2)**

5. Which of these alternate solutions do you think is best? Why?
Answers will vary. **(2)**

Name _____

What Can You Infer?

Read aloud the events listed from *The Wright Brothers: How They Invented the Airplane*. Use these quotes and your own experiences to complete the chart. Sample answers shown.

Story Event +	My Own Experience =	Inferences
Wilbur took the first turn to try to fly. Then Orville took the second turn.	People who take turns doing an important task are trying to be fair. **(2 points)**	The Wright brothers acted fairly toward each other. **(2)**
Five witnesses showed up to watch Orville try to fly.	When only five people show up to witness an event, the event is not very well known. **(2)**	Not many people were paying attention to the Wright brothers' efforts. **(2)**
Four and a half years passed from the time the Wright brothers wrote to the Smithsonian Institution until they had a successful flight.	People who work to accomplish a goal for four and a half years are very determined to succeed. **(2)**	The Wright brothers were very determined to make a successful flying machine. **(2)**

Assessment Tip: Total **12** Points

Name _____

Add an Ending

**Read the base words in the box. Then read the paragraphs. Add -*ed*
or -*ing* to a base word to form a word that completes each sentence.
Write the word in the blank.**

Word Bank

Base Words				
amuse	skip	drop	clap	agree
dance	dim	hate	prod	smile

Some word choices may vary. Sample answers shown.

At first, Sheila did not want to dance in the talent show.

"Last time I ___dropped__ **(1 point)** my hat and everyone thought

it was ___amusing__ **(1)**!" she said. "I just ___hated__ **(1)** it!"

All her friends kept ___prodding__ **(1)** her until she

___agreed__ **(1)** to try again.

This time when the lights ___dimmed__ **(1)**, Sheila

___skipped__ **(1)** onstage and ___danced__ **(1)** perfectly. She

___smiled__ **(1)** happily as the audience ___clapped__ **(1)** for her.

Assessment Tip: Total **10** Points

Name _____

What Else Does It Mean?

Read each sentence. Then use a different meaning for the underlined word to write a new sentence. Look in a dictionary to find another meaning for the word. Sample answers shown.

1. Marcos was <u>present</u> at my first surfing lesson.

   We bought him a wetsuit as a present. **(1 point)**

2. They <u>hike</u> the prices in that store every week.

   They will hike in the park this weekend. **(1)**

3. Harry hit his head on the door <u>frame</u>.

   She needs to frame her painting. **(1)**

4. The plane climbed a few <u>feet</u>.

   The water rushed over my feet. **(1)**

5. The girls fished along the <u>bank</u> of the river.

   He needs to put some money in the bank today. **(1)**

6. The plane <u>rose</u> into the air.

   Alice picked a rose from her garden. **(1)**

7. The plane's engine sputtered and <u>popped</u>.

   She popped a grape into her mouth. **(1)**

8. The surfers waited for another big <u>wave</u>.

   Joel raised his hand to wave at the surfers. **(1)**

Assessment Tip: Total **8** Points

Name _____

Spelling Review

Write Spelling Words from the list on this page to answer the questions. Order of answers in each category may vary.

1–9. Which nine words have the VCCCV pattern?

1. complain (**1 point**)
2. mischief (**1**)
3. countless (**1**)
4. laughter (**1**)
5. farther (**1**)
6. sandwich (**1**)
7. government (**1**)
8. improve (**1**)
9. address (**1**)

10–17. Which eight words have a VV pattern that makes two vowel sounds?

10. rodeo (**1**)
11. riot (**1**)
12. radio (**1**)
13. actual (**1**)
14. diary (**1**)
15. fuel (**1**)
16. cruel (**1**)
17. usual (**1**)

18–32. Which fifteen words have suffixes or end in *-ed* or *-ing*? Underline two words that also have the VCCCV pattern.

18. countless (**2**)
19. delightful (**1**)
20. actively (**1**)
21. lately (**1**)
22. government (**2**)
23. goodness (**1**)
24. watchful (**1**)
25. planned (**1**)
26. decided (**1**)
27. offered (**1**)
28. amusing (**1**)
29. hitting (**1**)
30. visiting (**1**)
31. covered (**1**)
32. ordered (**1**)

Spelling Words

1. complain
2. planned
3. mischief
4. countless
5. laughter
6. rodeo
7. decided
8. offered
9. delightful
10. farther
11. sandwich
12. actively
13. riot
14. amusing
15. radio
16. lately
17. government
18. actual
19. improve
20. goodness
21. hitting
22. diary
23. fuel
24. address
25. visiting
26. cruel
27. covered
28. watchful
29. usual
30. ordered

Theme 4: **Person to Person**   79
Assessment Tip: Total **34** Points

Name _____

Spelling Spree

Phrase Fillers **Write the Spelling Word that best completes each phrase.**

1. loud <u>laughter **(1 point)**</u> after a joke

2. working to <u>improve **(1)**</u> my grades

3. music on the <u>radio **(1)**</u>

4. a <u>countless **(1)**</u> number of stars

5. running out of <u>fuel **(1)**</u>

6. a cowboy starring in the <u>rodeo **(1)**</u>

7. a ham and cheese <u>sandwich **(1)**</u>

Word Detective **Use the following clues to figure out each Spelling Word. Write the word on the line.**

8. Not kind, but <u>cruel **(1)**</u>

9. Not out of the ordinary <u>usual **(1)**</u>

10. Tells where you live <u>address **(1)**</u>

11. A disturbance of the peace <u>riot **(1)**</u>

12. A daily written record <u>diary **(1)**</u>

13. Funny <u>amusing **(1)**</u>

14. The way a nation is ruled <u>government **(1)**</u>

15. Real, true, and factual <u>actual **(1)**</u>

Spelling Words

1. sandwich
2. cruel
3. address
4. actual
5. countless
6. government
7. laughter
8. amusing
9. fuel
10. usual
11. riot
12. diary
13. improve
14. rodeo
15. radio

Assessment Tip: Total **10** Points

Name _____

Proofreading and Writing

Proofreading Circle the six misspelled Spelling Words in this e-mail message. Then write each word correctly.

Dear Aunt Leslie and Uncle Alex,

My (goodnes!) I am excited about (visiding) you. Dad (orderd) me a new suitcase, so it has been hard (laitly) to wait until it is time to pack. I have been preparing (activly) for this vacation. I want to practice my pitching under Uncle Alex's (wachful) eye.

See you soon, Roy

1. goodness **(1 point)**   4. lately **(1)**

2. visiting **(1)**   5. actively **(1)**

3. ordered **(1)**   6. watchful **(1)**

Finish the Entry Complete the list by writing Spelling Words that make sense on the lines.

7. Uncle Alex offered **(1)** to help me with baseball.

8. We will practice hitting **(1)** baseballs.

9. Bring a gift for the party they have planned **(1)** .

10. I will be farther **(1)** from home than I've ever been.

11. Do not get into mischief **(1)** .

12. Bring my camera. Their beautiful garden will be covered **(1)** with flowers.

13. I have decided **(1)** to try fishing this year.

14. My aunt and uncle are delightful **(1)** people.

15. Don't complain **(1)** about anything.

✏— **Write a Letter** **On a separate sheet of paper, write a letter to someone you would like to visit. Use the Spelling Review Words.** Responses will vary. **(5)**

Assessment Tip: Total **20** Points

Using Comparative Forms of Adjectives

Complete each sentence with the correct form of the adjective in parentheses.

1. Yesterday was the ___warmest **(1 point)**___ day of the year. (warm)

2. The beach was ___warmer **(1)**___ than it was last week. (warm)

3. Noriko is a ___swifter **(1)**___ swimmer than I am. (swift)

4. Paolo is the ___swiftest **(1)**___ swimmer in our class. (swift)

5. Jana is a ___more careful **(1)**___ surfer than Daniel. (careful)

6. The ___most careful **(1)**___ surfer of all was Mika. (careful)

7. Greg is the ___most attentive **(1)**___ life guard on the beach. (attentive)

8. He is ___more attentive **(1)**___ than the head lifeguard is. (attentive)

9. Surfing is a ___more challenging **(1)**___ sport than ice skating is. (challenging)

10. It is the ___most challenging **(1)**___ sport I have tried. (challenging)

82   Theme 4: **Person to Person**

Assessment Tip: Total **10** Points

Name _____

Using Commas in Sentences

Add commas where they are needed.

1. Hand me my jacket, helmet, and goggles. **(1 point)**

2. Yes, takeoffs are dangerous. **(1)**

3. I do not fly in rain, hail, or snow. **(1)**

4. This is a biplane, George, not a triplane. **(1)**

5. The pilots of the first planes needed courage, skill, and good eyesight. **(1)**

6. Pilots carried maps, charts, and compasses with them. **(1)**

7. They used railroad tracks, roads, and rivers as guides. **(1)**

8. Friends, family members, and investors hoped for the best. **(1)**

9. Planes carried mail, parcels, and medicines to distant places. **(1)**

10. Well, Alvin, I'm not sure I want to fly in that plane. **(1)**

Assessment Tip: Total **10** Points

Name _____

Theater Terms

Use the words in the box to complete the theater critic's review.

The opening <u>performance</u> **(2 points)** of Jess T. Hack's new play, *You Call Me Paul,* was sold out. I can assure you that it won't be sold out again. The play was originally a 1940s television show, and I'll bet that the TV <u>version</u> **(2)** was much better. The <u>dialogue</u> **(2)** between the characters was dull, but they did the best they could with the lines they were given. It's too bad the <u>scenes</u> **(2)** weren't shorter, because every section of the play dragged on too long. The author of the <u>script</u> **(2)** should have spent more time fine tuning the play's plot and events. On a positive note, the <u>stage</u> **(2)** was beautifully decorated, and the actors moved around it quite well. In fact, these <u>stage directions</u> **(2)** made the play's action seem like a ballet, which was lovely to watch. All in all, though, I cannot recommend that anyone go to see this production.

Les Harsch
Theater Critic

Vocabulary

- dialogue
- performance
- scenes
- script
- stage
- stage directions
- version

Name _____

Plot Map: "The Case of the Runaway Appetite"

Complete the plot map. Tell what happens in each scene.

The problem: _A lost appetite needs to be found._ **(1 point)**

Scene	What Happens Sample answers
1	Joe hears that Veronica has lost her appetite. **(1)**
2	Joe convinces Veronica and Mrs. Bibby to let him help. **(1)**
3	They take off to find the appetite. **(1)**
4	They pick up the trail at the pizza parlor. **(1)**
5	They meet the police outside the mall. **(1)**
6	They find Appetite's footprints, and Veronica pursues her. **(1)**
7	Joe, Mrs. Bibby, and the police follow Veronica and her appetite into the Multiplex. **(1)**
8	The case is solved. **(1)**

Humor and Suspense

List examples of humor and suspense.

Humor	Suspenseful Moments
1. The idea of chasing down a lost appetite **(1)**	1. Whether Mrs. Bibby would let Joe help **(1)**
2. The appetite has green hair and an orange beret. **(1)**	2. Why Celia and Mario recognize Veronica's face **(1)**
3. The names of movies at the Multiplex **(1)**	3. What Veronica and Appetite are doing at the Multiplex **(1)**

Assessment Tip: Total **15** Points

Name _____

Comparing Productions

Think of a movie, play, or television show you have enjoyed. **Compare it to** *The Case of the Runaway Appetite.* **Make sure to think about the characters, the setting, the plot, and other details. In the Venn diagram below, use the intersecting part of the circles for the things that both productions have in common. Use the outer part of the circles to list the things that are different.**

Answers will vary. **(5 points** for each section of the diagram.**)**

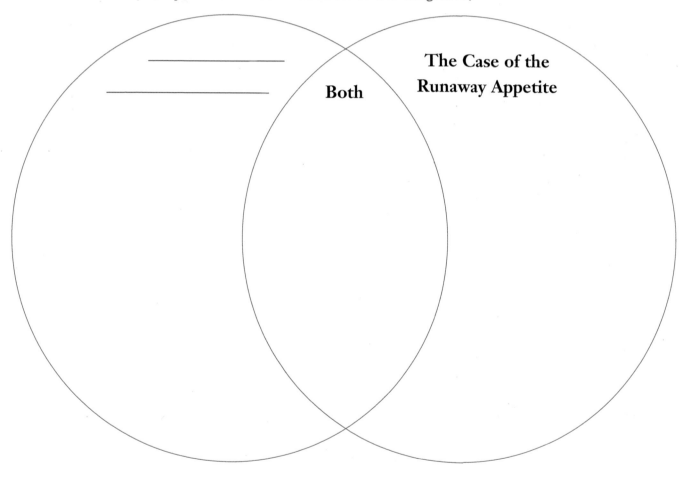

Both

The Case of the
Runaway Appetite

Name _____

Setting Up a Scene

Think about a sequel for *The Case of the Runaway Appetite* in which Joe Giles visits Princess Veronica in her own country. What would be the new setting for the opening scene? Which new characters would you introduce? What new problem could the characters face? Fill in a description of the setting, the characters, and the problem in the chart below. Be as precise as you can. Answers will vary.

Opening Scene	Description
Setting Time: Place:	(2 points)
Characters:	(4)
Problem:	(4)

Assessment Tip: Total **10** Points

Name _____

Analyzing Characters

Write a sentence that describes each character. Then support your answer with an example of something the character says or does.

Sample answers (**2 points** per character)

Character	Description	Example
Joe	Joe is outgoing, confident, and helpful.	He boldly offers his help to the princess.
Veronica	Veronica is energetic and adventuresome.	She chases Appetite at high speed at the mall and into the Multiplex.
Mrs. Bibby	Mrs. Bibby is cautious yet also fair.	She is slow to approve of Joe's ideas yet stands up for Joe with the police.
Sheriff McGrew	The sheriff is good-natured but feels superior and disinclined to respect young amateur detectives. He can open and change his mind.	The sheriff talks down to and pokes good-natured fun at Joe at first, but then listens to Joe and assists in the end.

Name _____

Detect the Patterns

Words with the VCCV pattern divide between the two consonants.
Words with VCV patterns may divide before or after the consonant.
Words with the VCCCV pattern divide either before or after the second
consonant. Words with the VV pattern divide between the vowels if the
vowels stand for two separate vowel sounds, as in *client: cli/ent*.

**Read each sentence below. Rewrite the underlined word with a slash
to divide the syllables. Then identify the word pattern: VCCV, VCV,
VCCCV, or VV.**

1. That sweater must be hidden somewhere in my messy <u>closet</u>.
   clos/et VCV **(1 point)**

2. I need to clean my <u>entire</u> room soon. en/tire VCCV **(1)**

3. Dad says if I <u>valued</u> my belongings more, I'd take better care of them.
   val/ued VCV **(1)**

4. I <u>explained</u> that this was not the real problem. ex/plained VCCCV **(1)**

5. The <u>real</u> issue is lack of space. re/al VV **(1)**

6. My <u>complete</u> collection of Red Sox memorabilia, for example, takes up
   18 shoeboxes. com/plete VCCCV **(1)**

7. And where am I supposed to put my <u>giant</u> replica of the first space shuttle?
   gi/ant VV **(1)**

8. I need an <u>entire</u> floor of the house for my stuff. en/tire VCCV **(1)**

9. I'll have to <u>approach</u> my parents with this proposition. ap/proach VCCCV **(1)**

10. If they say yes, my little sister will have to move to a <u>hotel</u>.
    ho/tel VCV **(1)**

Assessment Tip: Total **10** Points

Name _____

Unusual Spellings

Some words have vowel or consonant sounds spelled with
unusual spelling patterns. The spellings of these words have to
be remembered.

**Write the Spelling Words. Underline the unusual spelling
pattern in each word.** Order of answers may vary.

guy **(1 point)**

either **(1)**

character **(1)**

machine **(1)**

biscuit **(1)**

scene **(1)**

choir **(1)**

young **(1)**

scent **(1)**

chorus **(1)**

threaten **(1)**

tangerine **(1)**

plaid **(1)**

journal **(1)**

cello **(1)**

scheme **(1)**

southern **(1)**

muscle **(1)**

guarantee **(1)**

typical **(1)**

1. guy
2. either
3. character
4. machine
5. biscuit
6. scene
7. choir
8. young
9. scent
10. chorus
11. threaten
12. tangerine
13. plaid
14. journal
15. cello
16. scheme
17. southern
18. muscle
19. guarantee
20. typical

Assessment Tip: Total **20** Points

Name _____

Spelling Spree

Analogies An **analogy** shows two pairs of words that have the same relationship, such as synonyms, opposites, or a word and a category in which that word belongs.

Write the Spelling Word that completes each analogy.

1. *Hot* is to *cold* as *old* is to <u>young **(1 point)**</u> .

2. *Trumpet* is to *tuba* as *violin* is to <u>cello **(1)**</u> .

3. *Thought* is to *brain* as *strength* is to <u>muscle **(1)**</u> .

4. *Ship* is to *boat* as *diary* is to <u>journal **(1)**</u> .

5. *East* is to *west* as *northern* is to <u>southern **(1)**</u> .

6. *Ear* is to *sound* as *nose* is to <u>scent **(1)**</u> .

7. *Horse* is to *pony* as *orange* is to <u>tangerine **(1)**</u> .

8. *Woman* is to *man* as *gal* is to <u>guy **(1)**</u> .

Word Clues **Write a Spelling Word to fit each clue.**

9. a plan	9. <u>scheme **(1)**</u>
10. one or the other	10. <u>either **(1)**</u>
11. a person in a play or story	11. <u>character **(1)**</u>
12. a promise	12. <u>guarantee **(1)**</u>
13. normal or average	13. <u>typical **(1)**</u>
14. tasty baked dough	14. <u>biscuit **(1)**</u>
15. a clothing pattern	15. <u>plaid **(1)**</u>

Assessment Tip: Total **15** Points

Spelling Words

1. guy
2. either
3. character
4. machine
5. biscuit
6. scene
7. choir
8. young
9. scent
10. chorus
11. threaten
12. tangerine
13. plaid
14. journal
15. cello
16. scheme
17. southern
18. muscle
19. guarantee
20. typical

Proofreading and Writing

Proofreading Circle the five misspelled Spelling Words in this
part of a script. Then write each word correctly.
Order of answers may vary.

Spelling Words

(In this (sceen,) Tim, Kyle, and Gus are standing on the front steps
of a large downtown church. Music and singing can be heard
coming from inside.)

Kyle: We're going to have to go in there and find the stolen
(macheen) ourselves.

Gus: I'm not going in there to search around the feet of a
bunch of (korous) singers! Besides, why would Max
Devlin have stashed the device in the middle of a
church (quire?)

Tim: You're going in if I have to carry you myself, Gus.

Gus: Don't (thretan) me, Tim. *(To Kyle)* Who does this guy
think he is?

Kyle: You two can either stop fighting or go home, OK?
(Gus and Tim hang their heads, embarrassed) We can't
underestimate Max Devlin's cunning. We have to
search the church. Let's go!

1. guy
2. either
3. character
4. machine
5. biscuit
6. scene
7. choir
8. young
9. scent
10. chorus
11. threaten
12. tangerine
13. plaid
14. journal
15. cello
16. scheme
17. southern
18. muscle
19. guarantee
20. typical

1. __**(1 point)** scene__   4. __**(1)** choir__

2. __**(1)** machine__   5. __**(1)** threaten__

3. __**(1)** chorus__

**On a separate sheet of paper, write a paragraph giving your prediction of what will
happen next in the play. Use Spelling Words from the list.**

Responses will vary. **(5 points)**

Name _____

What I Mean Is....

Each sentence below contains a common idiom. Rewrite each sentence, replacing the idiom with a word or phrase that means the same thing. Answers will vary. Sample answers shown. **(1 point** each)

1. When my sister told me to <u>go fly a kite</u>, I got mad and slammed the door.

   When my sister told me to go away, I got mad and slammed the door.

2. Later on, she asked me to <u>lend her a hand</u> with a heavy box of books.

   Later on, she asked me to help her with a heavy box of books.

3. I told her to <u>use a little elbow grease</u> and do it herself.

   I told her to make a little effort and do it herself.

4. That really made her <u>lose it</u>!

   That really made her mad!

5. Mildred and I seldom <u>see eye-to-eye</u> on any issue.

   Mildred and I seldom have the same opinion on any issue.

6. When we're <u>on the outs</u>, though, I miss her company.

   When we're not getting along, though, I miss her company.

7. Our parents are very <u>well heeled</u>, and we own several vacation homes.

   Our parents are rich, and we own several vacation homes.

8. I think they've <u>lost their marbles</u>, though, because they want to become shell collectors in Tahiti. I think they've gone crazy, though, because they want to become shell collectors in Tahiti.

9. Meanwhile, my brother has been <u>sitting on top of the world</u> since he got accepted to art school. Meanwhile, my brother has been very happy since he got accepted to art school.

10. I think he has <u>too many irons in the fire</u>, though, since he also wants to become a doctor, a dentist, and a horse trainer.

    I think he's attempting too many things, though, since he also wants to become a doctor, a dentist, and a horse trainer.

Name _____

The School Fair

More Commas in a Series **Use commas to set off three or more sentences in a series.**

Jan scrubbed, Teke mopped, and Shaya picked up clutter.

Add commas to separate sentences in a series. Write each sentence correctly.

1. The parents held a fund-raising auction the fifth-grade class performed a play and the chorus led a sing-along.

   The parents held a fund-raising auction, the fifth-grade class performed a play,

   and the chorus led a sing-along. **(2 points)**

2. Teachers organized contests the principal held relay races and volunteers planned a picnic.

   Teachers organized contests, the principal led relay races, and volunteers

   planned a picnic. **(2)**

3. Third-graders brought salads fourth-graders made sandwiches and fifth-graders baked desserts.

   Third-graders brought salads, fourth-graders made sandwiches, and

   fifth-graders baked desserts. **(2)**

4. The newspaper sent a reporter the fire chief brought a fire engine and the mayor stopped by.

   The newspaper sent a reporter, the fire chief brought a fire engine, and the

   mayor stopped by. **(2)**

5. The principal handed out awards Mr. Bailey made a video and Ms. Filmore wrote an article for the newspaper.

   The principal handed out awards, Mr. Bailey made a video, and Ms. Filmore

   wrote an article for the newspaper. **(2)**

Assessment Tip: Total **10** Points

Signs of the Times

More Abbreviations Most abbreviations begin with a capital letter and
end with a period, but not all do.

in. = inch	**ht.** = height	**cm** = centimeter	**mph** = miles per hour
ft. = foot or feet	**wt.** = weight	**kg** = kilogram	**mpg** = miles per gallon
yd. = yard	**lb.** = pound		

Write the correct abbreviations for the underlined words in these ads.

1. Deli Special Today!
   Roast turkey $3.49 <u>pound</u>

   lb. **(1 point)** _____

2. All Velvet Ribbon
   $1.79 <u>yard</u>

   yd. **(1)** _____

3. Try out the new Tooter Scooter!
   Speeds up to 20 <u>miles per hour</u>
   Up to 60 <u>miles per gallon</u>

   mph **(1)** _____

   mpg **(1)** _____

4. GOLD CHAINS CUT TO ANY LENGTH
   $2.50 <u>inch</u> or $25 <u>foot</u>

   in. **(1)** _____   ft. **(1)** _____

Application for Library Card

1. Name *Morris Raimey*

2. Address *1302 West 8th St., St. Louis, MO*

3. Age *11*

4. Color of eyes *brown*

5. <u>Height</u> *51 centimeters*

6. <u>Weight</u> *40 kilograms*

ht. **(1)** _____

cm **(1)** _____

wt **(1)** _____

kg **(1)** _____

Assessment Tip: Total **10** Points

Name _____

The Search

Using Commas Correctly Use commas to set off introductory words and phrases, mild interjections, and nouns in direct address. Also, use commas to separate the parts of a compound sentence and items in a series, including a series of sentences.

Use proofreading marks to correct nine missing commas, a missing apostrophe, a missing exclamation mark, an incorrect end mark, and two words that need capital letters in this play dialogue. (**1 point** for each correction)

Example: Help, I need a Detective.

Brad: Can you help me find something Detective grubb?

Detective Grubb: Yes Brad I can help you find *anything!*

Brad: Wow that's good news! I need you to find space for my ant farm my swimming trophies, and my jigsaw puzzle.

Detective Grubb: Put the ant farm where those old sneakers are clear away the papers on your desk for the puzzle and stack the books on your shelves to make room for the trophies.

Brad: There's not enough space.

Detective Grubb: You just need to be more organized or you need to give away things you dont use.

Brad: Hey I asked you to *find* space rather than *make* space.

Detective Grubb: Sometimes I *find* you *very* trying Brad!

Name _____

Planning a Play

Fill in the boxes to plan writing a play.   Answers will vary.

Characters	(2 points)
Setting	(2)
Plot: What Happens	
Problem	(2)
Opening scene	(2)
Middle events	(2)
Ending (how problem is solved)	(2)

Assessment Tip: Total **12** Points

Name _____

Using Exact Verbs

In this passage from a play, Elmo is frantically getting ready for baseball practice. Read the stage directions beside each space. Write an exact verb in the space provided. Answers may vary. **(2 points** each)

Characters: Elmo and his sister Alice

Setting: Elmo's messy bedroom

Elmo: (_sorting_____ *through a pile of clothes and sports gear)* Where on earth is my baseball glove?

Alice: (_pointing_____ *to a different pile)* Somewhere under the mountain of stuff on your bedroom floor, I suppose.

Elmo: Alice, help me find the glove! Practice begins in fifteen minutes, and I need it!

Alice: (_lifting_____ *the pillow)* Here it is! Under your pillow!

Elmo: (_grinning_____ *with relief)* I remember! I put it there to help me dream of baseball.

Alice: Okay. You'd better hurry.

Elmo: (_grabbing_____ *the glove)* I'm off!

Name _____

One Land, Many Trails

After reading each selection, complete the chart to show what you learned about the people who lived on the American frontier long ago.

	Pioneer Girl	**A Boy Called Slow**
Tell who the main character in this selection is, and give one important fact about that person.	The main character is Grace McCance. She was a young girl in a pioneer family that settled on the prairie. **(2.5 points)**	The main character is a boy named Slow. He was a member of the Lakota Sioux people, who lived on the Great Plains. **(2.5)**
What special challenges did this person face in the selection?	Grace faced harsh living conditions, fierce storms, prairie fires, and difficult chores. **(2.5)**	Slow had to earn a new name for himself by doing something brave or outstanding. **(2.5)**
What traits helped this person successfully overcome the challenges?	Grace was willing to do whatever was asked of her. She was brave in the face of dangers and made the best of her situation. **(2.5)**	Slow's determination helped him develop skills and strength. He showed courage and quick thinking in the battle that earned him the name Sitting Bull. **(2.5)**
How did this person's efforts contribute to America's past?	Grace and her family helped settle the Great Plains. **(2.5)**	Slow became a great leader of the Sioux. **(2.5)**

Assessment Tip: Total **10** Points per selection and **2** points for the final question

Name _____

One Land, Many Trails continued

	Black Cowboy Wild Horses	**Elena**
Tell who the main character in this selection is, and give one important fact about that person.	Bob Lemmons is the main character. He was an African American cowboy who was an expert at catching wild mustangs. **(2.5)**	Elena is the main character. She was born in Mexico and had to flee to the United States to escape a war. **(2.5)**
What special challenges did this person face in the selection?	Bob had the difficult job of catching wild mustangs. He had to find the mustangs by tracking them and then get the herds to follow him. **(2.5)**	Elena lost her husband at a young age. She had children to care for. She had to leave her home and make a new life in a new land. **(2.5)**
What traits helped this person successfully overcome the challenges?	Bob understood mustangs. He had the special talent of getting the horses to believe he was one of them. He was clever and brave. **(2.5)**	Elena was strong and steady. She knew what she needed to do and she did it. Her hard work helped her children thrive in America. **(2.5)**
How did this person's efforts contribute to America's past?	He helped other cowboys do their jobs by obtaining horses for them. **(2.5)**	She helped settle California and make that part of the country grow. **(2.5)**

What have you learned about the contributions different people have made to America's culture and heritage?

Sample answer: I learned that people from many different cultural

backgrounds and from many different places contributed to America's

growth. I learned that our diverse culture began on the frontier.

Assessment Tip: Total **10** Points per selection and **2** points for the final question

Name _____

Path of the Warrior

Read the paragraph below. Use the words in the box to fill in the blanks.

> **Vocabulary**
>
> customs
> reputation
> inherited
> raid
> extended
> vision
> determination
> respect

Physical abilities are mostly <u>inherited **(1 point)**</u> from parents and grandparents, but character is developed through life experiences. How could a young brave earn a <u>reputation **(1)**</u> as a courageous warrior? One way was to lead a <u>raid **(1)**</u> against an enemy camp. Another was to engage a rival group in battle and touch their leader with a coup stick. Still another was to show <u>determination **(1)**</u> in completing a difficult mission. Earning the <u>respect **(1)**</u> of both the <u>extended **(1)**</u> family and the tribal elders was very important to young braves. This could only be done by faithfully observing the traditions and <u>customs **(1)**</u> of the people. One important tradition was going alone on a wilderness journey to seek a <u>vision **(1)**</u>. Sometimes this would provide the brave with a new name, one that carried strength and power.

Name ______________________________

Conclusions Chart

Story Clues	+		=	Conclusions
page 471 Returns Again and his wife give thanks when a son is born. **(2 points)**	+	Returns Again hopes his son will hunt for the people and protect them. **(2)**	=	The boy is born into a loving family who will help him grow up to be strong and brave. **(2)**
pages 472–475 As Slow grows up, he is unhappy with his name. He wishes for a vision of bravery. **(2)**	+	Slow admires his father's courage, wisdom, and bravery. **(2)**	=	Slow probably has the makings of a good leader.
pages 476–479 Slow wrestles and practices hunting. He becomes strong. He kills a buffalo at age ten.	+	Slow is careful and deliberate. People stop teasing him. He decides to join a battle against the Crow.	=	Slow has grown to be strong, confident, and skilled—maybe he is old enough to become a warrior. **(2)**
pages 480–483 Slow announces that he will join the raid. Instead of waiting, he races ahead toward the Crow.	+	Slow touches a Crow warrior with his coup stick and knocks an arrow out of his hand. The Crow warriors flee.	=	Slow is daring and brave, and he shows skill as a warrior. **(2)**

What predictions can you make about the kind of person Slow will grow up to be?

Answers will vary. **(2)**

Assessment Tip: Total **16** Points

Name _____

Slow's Early Life in a Line

The timeline below shows some important events in Sitting Bull's early life. Answer each question to tell about each event.

1. **1831:**
   Who has a son?

2. **First Months of Life:**
   What name do Returns Again and his wife give their son? Why?

3. **Age Seven:**
   How does Slow feel about his name? What does he dream of?

4. **The Hunting Trip:**
   What happens when Returns Again goes hunting?

5. **Age Ten:**
   What big thing does Slow do? What else does he do to prepare himself for adulthood?

6. **Age Fourteen:**
   What does Slow decide to do? What happens as a result?

1. Returns Again's wife gives birth to a son. **(2 points)**

2. They name him Slow because he does everything slowly. **(2)**

3. Slow doesn't like his name. He dreams that a vision of bravery will come to him, a vision that would allow him to prove himself to his people. **(2)**

4. A big bull buffalo speaks four powerful names to Returns Again. **(2)**

5. At the age of ten, Slow kills his first buffalo. He also hunts with his bow and arrows, races his gray pony, and wrestles with his friends. **(2)**

6. Slow goes with his father to fight the Crow. He leads the attack. The Crow warriors flee. Slow is a hero and he gets a new name: Sitting Bull. **(2)**

Name _____

Why Do You Think . . . ?

Read the following passage. Then complete the activity on page 107.

Sequoyah

When he was a child, few people would have guessed that Sequoyah would one day be hailed as a genius and a savior of the Cherokee nation. He was born around 1760 and grew up in Tennessee, following Cherokee customs and wearing the traditional dress of the Cherokee people. A childhood illness left him partially disabled, but he managed to acquire the skills of a silversmith and blacksmith.

Sequoyah never learned to speak, read, or write in English. However, he became fascinated with English writing. In fact, he believed that the secret of the white settlers' success was their written language.

Sequoyah figured out that each letter in the English alphabet represented a sound. In 1809 he set out to create a similar alphabet for the Cherokee language. On scraps of tree bark, he scratched symbols to stand for the sounds of Cherokee. His wife did not approve.

"Why are you wasting your time?" she complained. "You should be working, not drawing pictures!"

Sequoyah ignored her. He knew that his work could be important for the Cherokee people. Finally, after many years, he had created a set of eighty-five characters to represent all the sounds of the Cherokee language. When he showed the members of his tribe, however, they laughed at him.

"What do we need an alphabet for?" they said.

Sequoyah didn't lose faith, though. He traveled to Georgia to show his work to the top Cherokee chiefs. They were impressed. The alphabet was easy to learn, and it allowed people to communicate in writing. Soon, the Cherokee were publishing their own newspaper. Sequoyah was praised as a great man by both the Cherokee and the American government. He became a teacher and a highly respected leader of the Cherokee people.

Name _____

Why Do You Think . . .? continued

Answer these questions about the passage on page 106.

Sample answers shown.

1. Why do you think Sequoyah was considered a genius?

   He created an entirely new alphabet even though he had had no

   formal education. **(2 points)**

2. In what ways might the Cherokee alphabet have helped to preserve

   Cherokee customs and ways of life?

   It allowed people to write about their customs and traditions

   so they wouldn't be forgotten. **(2)**

3. Why do you think Sequoyah continued working on the alphabet

   despite the fact that other members of his tribe did not approve?

   Maybe he knew the alphabet would be useful and important. **(2)**

   _____

4. Why do you think the Cherokee people changed their minds about

   the alphabet?

   Once they saw how useful the alphabet was they understood its

   importance. **(2)**

5. What character traits did Sequoyah possess? Use details from the

   passage to help you answer.

   Examples: He was very smart because he created an alphabet; he

   was an independent thinker because he carried on despite the

   disapproval of others; he was persistent because he worked on the

   alphabet for many years. **(2)**

Name _____

Word Parts Match

Read each sentence. Match a prefix or suffix from the box on the left with a base word from the box on the right to form a word that completes the sentence. Write the word in the blank. (The prefixes and suffix may be used more than once.)

dis- in- -ion
re- un-

accurate	agreed	aware	cooperate
direct	like	possess	turned

1. As they grew older, many of the boys began to <u>dislike **(1 point)**</u> their childhood names and wish for new ones.

2. Returns Again earned his name when he <u>returned **(1)**</u> to protect his people from an enemy raid.

3. The low rumbling noise came from the <u>direction **(1)**</u> of the trail.

4. Returns Again <u>disagreed **(1)**</u> with the others, who wanted to take out their weapons.

5. Unlike Returns Again, the other men were <u>unaware **(1)**</u> of what the big bull buffalo's sounds meant.

6. Slow struck the Crow warrior's arm with his coup stick to make his aim <u>inaccurate **(1)**</u>.

7. After their victory, the Lakota Sioux warriors took <u>possession **(1)**</u> of the enemy's horses and weapons.

8. Their spirit of <u>cooperation **(1)**</u> helped the Lakota Sioux people provide for and protect each other.

Assessment Tip: Total **8** Points

Name _____

Words with a Prefix or a Suffix (un-, dis-, in-, re-; -ion)

A **prefix** is a word part added to the beginning of a base word or a word root. It adds meaning to a word. Some of the Spelling Words contain the prefixes *un-*, *dis-*, *in-*, or *re-*. To spell these words, find the prefix and the base word or the word root.

Prefix + Base Word: **un**able   **dis**cover

Prefix + Word Root: **re**port   **in**spect

A **suffix** is a word part added to the end of a base word. The suffix *-ion* can change verbs into nouns. When a verb ends with *e*, drop the *e* and add *-ion*. If a verb does not end with *e*, just add *-ion*.

VERB: promote   react   NOUN: promot**ion**   react**ion**

Write the Spelling Words. Underline the prefixes *un-*, *dis-*, *in-*, and *re-*. Circle the suffix *-ion*.

Order of responses for each category may vary.

<u>un</u>able **(1)**	<u>re</u>act **(1)**
<u>dis</u>cover **(1)**	<u>re</u>act(ion) **(1)**
<u>re</u>port **(1)**	tense **(1)**
<u>dis</u>aster **(1)**	tens(ion) **(1)**
<u>un</u>aware **(1)**	correct **(1)**
<u>re</u>mind **(1)**	correct(ion) **(1)**
televise **(1)**	promote **(1)**
televis(ion) **(1)**	promot(ion) **(1)**
<u>in</u>spect **(1)**	express **(1)**
<u>in</u>spect(ion) **(1)**	express(ion) **(1)**

Spelling Words

1. unable
2. discover
3. report
4. disaster
5. unaware
6. remind
7. televise
8. television
9. inspect
10. inspection
11. react
12. reaction
13. tense
14. tension
15. correct
16. correction
17. promote
18. promotion
19. express
20. expression

Name _____

Spelling Spree

Meaning Match Write the Spelling Word that has each meaning and word part below.

1. unable
2. discover
3. report
4. disaster
5. unaware
6. remind
7. televise
8. television
9. inspect
10. inspection
11. react
12. reaction
13. tense
14. tension
15. correct
16. correction
17. promote
18. promotion
19. express
20. expression

1. to examine + *ion*
2. *dis* + a container lid
3. to broadcast + *ion*
4. *re* + to do something
5. to make right + *ion*
6. *un* + capable of doing something
7. nervous + *ion*
8. to move to a higher position + *ion*

dis **+**

1. inspection **(1 point)**
2. discover **(1)**
3. television **(1)**
4. react **(1)**
5. correction **(1)**
6. unable **(1)**
7. tension **(1)**
8. promotion **(1)**

Hidden Words Write the Spelling Word that is hidden in each row of letters. Don't let the other words fool you!

9. c o r e a c t i o n c e
10. g l e e x p r e s s u r e
11. c h a i n s p e c t r i p
12. a r c o r r e c t a n g l e

13. h o t e l e v i s e n s e
14. d a m p r o m o t e a m
15. h a r d i s a s t e r n

9. reaction **(1)**
10. express **(1)**
11. inspect **(1)**
12. correct **(1)**

13. televise **(1)**
14. promote **(1)**
15. disaster **(1)**

Assessment Tip: Total **15** Points

Name _____

Proofreading and Writing

Circle the five misspelled Spelling Words in this part of a script for a class play. Then write each word correctly.

Spelling Words

Slow: How much longer will we have to be called by these

names? Every time I hear mine, all it does is (remined)

me that the elders think of me as just a child. These

days, whenever anyone calls my name, I get very (tens.)

Hungry Mouth: I know what you mean. I have the same

reaction. I'd like a name that's an (expresion) of something

more than the fact that I have a big appetite. But what

can we do? It's not like the elders are (unawear) of our

feelings.

Slow: That's true, but they're still waiting for us to do

something worthy of a new name. The next time they

form a war party we should (repport) for duty.

1. unable
2. discover
3. report
4. disaster
5. unaware
6. remind
7. televise
8. television
9. inspect
10. inspection
11. react
12. reaction
13. tense
14. tension
15. correct
16. correction
17. promote
18. promotion
19. express
20. expression

1. remind **(1 point)**   4. unaware **(1)**

2. tense **(1)**   5. report **(1)**

3. expression **(1)**

▸ **Write a Summary** If a friend were to ask you what *A Boy Called Slow* is about, what would you say? What happens in the story? Who are the main characters? What details are most important in understanding the events of the story?

On a separate piece of paper, write a brief summary of the story. Use Spelling Words from the list. Responses will vary. **(5)**

Name _____

Slow Is to Boy as . . .

Read each analogy. Write the word that best completes each analogy.

1. *Share* is to *hoard* as *gain* is to <u>lose **(1)**</u>.
   collect   lose   heavy   surrender

2. *Inherited* is to *received* as *yelled* is to <u>shouted **(1)**</u>.
   hushed   anger   argued   shouted

3. *Son* is to *relative* as *pony* is to <u>animal **(1)**</u>.
   mane   saddle   animal   stirrups

4. *Courage* is to *warriors* as *wisdom* is to <u>elders **(1)**</u>.
   elders   infants   smart   college

5. *Retreat* is to *advance* as *speak* is to <u>listen **(1)**</u>.
   chatter   listen   silent   command

6. *Slow* is to *name* as *winter* is to <u>season **(1)**</u>.
   summer   frozen   snow   season

7. *Follow* is to *trail* as *protect* is to <u>guard **(1)**</u>.
   guard   warn   attack   watch

Use any three of the words in the box to write an incomplete analogy on a separate piece of paper. Challenge a partner to complete it with one of the remaining words. Sample answer shown.

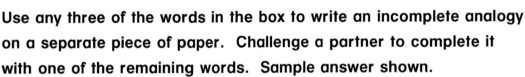

climb	deep	flat	mountains
oceans	peaked	plains	swim

8. *Plains* is to *flat* as *mountains* is to *peaked*. **(1)**

Assessment Tip: Total **8** Points

Name _____

We Object to It

Subject and Object Pronouns A pronoun is a word that replaces a noun. *I, you, he, she, it, we,* and *they* are subject pronouns. *Me, you, him, her, it, us,* and *them* are object pronouns. Use a subject pronoun as the subject of a sentence or after forms of *be.* Use an object pronoun as the object of an action verb or after words like *to, for,* or *with.*

Underline the pronoun in parentheses that correctly completes each sentence.

1. (I/me) have a nickname. **(1 point)**

2. My family gave (I/me) the nickname Skeeter. **(1)**

3. My brother Michael is called Apple because (he/him) has red cheeks. **(1)**

4. People give apples to (he/him) all the time. **(1)**

5. (They/Them) think Michael always wants an apple. **(1)**

6. My sister Cheryl is called Cookie by (we/us). **(1)**

7. Everyone gives cookies to (she/her). **(1)**

8. If anyone likes cookies, it is (she/her). **(1)**

9. Cheryl thanks (they/them). **(1)**

10. Michael and Cheryl share apples and cookies with (we/us). **(1)**

Name _____

Should It Be *I* or *Me*?

Using *I* and *Me* Use *I* as the subject of a sentence and after forms of *be*.
Use *me* after action verbs and after words like *to*, *in*, *for*, and *with*. When
using the pronouns *I* and *me* with nouns or other pronouns, name
yourself last.

Incorrect:	**Jack and me** went to the movies.
Incorrect:	**I and Jack** went to the movies.
Correct:	**Jack and I** went to the movies.
Incorrect:	That was a treat for **Jack and I**.
Incorrect:	That was a treat for **me and Jack**.
Correct:	That was a treat for **Jack and me**.

**Underline the words in parentheses that correctly complete each
sentence. (1 point each)**

1. (Latisha and I/Latisha and me) found shiny, black arrowheads near
   the creek.
2. (She and I/Her and me) went to the library to learn about
   arrowheads.
3. The librarian told (Latisha and I/Latisha and me) that our
   arrowheads were made of obsidian, a kind of volcanic glass.
4. (You and I/You and me) should meet Latisha at the creek tomorrow.
5. Another discovery would be fun for (Latisha and I/Latisha and me).
6. If Latisha finds one, she will give it to (you and me/you and I).
7. (Her and I/She and I) have found broken arrowheads before.
8. But yesterday (I and she/she and I) found two perfect specimens!
9. The arrowhead collection gathered by (her and me/she and I) is
   growing.
10. Soon (she and I/her and me) will have the largest collection around.

Assessment Tip: Total **10** Points

Name _____

We're Pronoun Pros

Good writers are careful to use a subject pronoun as the subject of a sentence or after a form of *be*. They use an object pronoun after an action verb and after a word like *to, for, with,* or *in.*

Gloria is writing for the school newspaper. Proofread her draft. Cross out each incorrect pronoun or pronoun phrase and write the correct pronoun or phrase above it. (1 point each)

                                                    I

Last Saturday, George, Nan, Kathy, and ~~me~~ followed a trail

                                 I

in the woods on Prospect Hill. Kathy and ~~me~~ asked George and

                               him   her

Nan to lead us. The hiking club gave ~~he~~ and ~~she~~ trailblazing badges.

Kathy and I

~~I and Kathy~~ knew they would keep us on the path. George knew a

                                         he

special place at the end of the trail. It was ~~him~~ who suggested the hike.

The trail was thick with brambles, but George and Nan kept us on

                                    he   she

the right path. After half an hour of walking, ~~him~~ and ~~her~~ called out to

               me

Kathy and ~~I~~. The sun shone brightly on wildflowers and bushes full of

                                            them

fat, juicy blackberries. George picked four berries and washed ~~they~~ with

                                             her

water. Nan held out her hand and George gave one berry to ~~she~~ and one

                                        We

to each of us. Nothing has ever tasted so good. ~~Us~~ will go back soon!

Name _____

Writing a Speech

In *A Boy Called Slow*, a fourteen-year-old Lakota boy courageously protects his people from a Crow war party and earns himself a new name. His father, Returns Again, gives a very brief **speech** about Slow's bravery. Now you will write your own speech. Choose one of the topics listed below.

► Write a speech in which Returns Again describes his son's courage in the battle against the Crow and announces his son's new name.

► Write a speech about a current topic that you feel strongly about.

Use the chart below to help you get started. First, identify the purpose of your speech — to entertain, to persuade, to thank, or to inform — and the audience to whom you will deliver it. Then jot down specific examples you might include to support your main idea. Before you begin writing, number your examples, beginning with *1*, **to arrange the order in which you will present them.**

Purpose	Audience	Examples
(3 points)	(3)	(3)

Write your speech on a separate sheet of paper. First, mention whom you are addressing and what the purpose of your speech is. Then present your ideas in a logical order. Be sure to use emotional words and powerful examples that help make your point. Finally, end with a conclusion that sums up or restates the purpose. When you finish, deliver your speech to the class. (6 points)

Assessment Tip: Total **15** Points

Name _____

Using Quotations

Good speechwriters make their speeches more lively and powerful by including **direct quotations** made by people who have something important to say about the topic. When you use a direct quotation in your own writing, make sure to do the following:

► Write the exact words the person said.

► Use quotation marks to separate the direct quotation from the rest of the sentence.

► Give the name of the person who is responsible for the quotation.

► Check that the spelling of the quoted person's name is correct.

Carefully read these quotations by well-known Native Americans.

> "We do not want riches, we want peace and love."
> —*Chief Red Cloud*

> "The earth and myself are of one mind."
> —*Chief Joseph*

Now proofread the speech excerpts in which these quotations are used. On the lines, rewrite each excerpt to correct the speechwriters' use of quotations. Use the guidelines listed above to help you.

1. Scott Franklin will now share remarkable slides of his round-the-world camping trip. Mr. Franklin's experiment in living echoes Cheif Josef's belief that The earth and myself are of one mind.

   Scott Franklin will now share remarkable slides of his round-the-world

   camping trip. Mr. Franklin's experiment in living echoes **Chief**

   Joseph's belief that "The earth and myself are of one mind." **(4 points)**

2. Our neighborhood group opposes the proposed development because, as someone said, We do not want riches, we want peace and love.

   Our neighborhood group opposes the proposed development

   because, as **Chief Red Cloud** said, "We do not want riches, we want

   peace and love." **(4)**

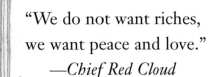

Revising Your Research Report

Reread your research report. Put a checkmark in the box for each sentence that describes your paper. Use this page to help you revise.

Rings the Bell

☐ My report tells many facts about one clear, focused topic.

☐ I wrote one paragraph with a topic sentence for each main idea.

☐ I wrote in my own words. I used descriptive language.

☐ I included an introduction, a conclusion, and a list of sources.

☐ My sentences flow well. There are almost no mistakes.

Getting Stronger

☐ My report could be more focused. I need to do more research.

☐ My paragraphs need topic sentences. Some facts are out of place.

☐ I didn't always use my own words. I need more exact words.

☐ I need an introduction, a conclusion, or a list of sources.

☐ Some sentences are choppy. There are some mistakes.

Try Harder

☐ My report is not focused on a topic. There are almost no facts.

☐ Main ideas are not organized into paragraphs with topic sentences.

☐ The introduction, the conclusion, and the source list are missing.

☐ I rarely used my own words. There are no exact words.

☐ Most sentences are choppy. There are many mistakes.

Name _____

Pronoun Reference

Pronouns are words that replace nouns or other words. Write the word or words that the underlined pronoun refers to in each exercise.

1. Gems are hard to find. <u>They</u> are usually embedded in ordinary-looking rocks.

2. Without impurities, gems would be colorless crystals. The color of a gem depends on the type of impurities <u>it</u> contains.

3. The metal chromium gives a green color to one kind of crystal, turning <u>it</u> into an emerald.

4. Gems can be harder than the rock that surrounds <u>them</u>.

5. Rock hunters often find gems in riverbeds. <u>They</u> look for places where the surrounding rock has been eroded away.

6. Sapphires are a fiery blue. <u>They</u> get their color from a mixture of titanium and iron.

7. Rubies have chromium as an impurity. It gives <u>them</u> a deep red color.

8. Once a gem is found, <u>it</u> must be cut by gem-cutters.

1. gems **(1 point)** _____

2. gem **(1)** _____

3. crystal **(1)** _____

4. gems **(1)** _____

5. rock hunters **(1)** _____

6. sapphires **(1)** _____

7. rubies **(1)** _____

8. gem **(1)** _____

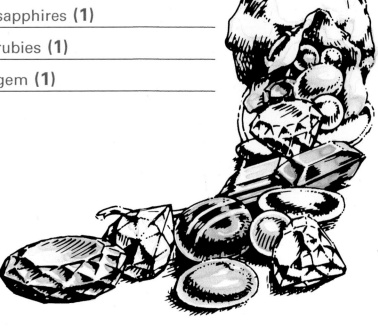

Name _____

Spelling Words

Words Often Misspelled Look for familiar spelling patterns to help you remember how to spell the Spelling Words on this page. Think carefully about the parts that you find hard to spell in each word.

Write the missing letters in the Spelling Words below.

1. w ___ h ___ ile **(1 point)**

2. w ___ h ___ ole **(1)**

3. a ___ n ___ y ___ way **(1)**

4. a ___ n y ___ one **(1)**

5. a ___ n y ___ thing **(1)**

6. favor i ___ t ___ e ___ **(1)**

7. on c ___ e ___ **(1)**

8. su p ___ p ___ ose **(1)**

9. ev e ___ r ___ y ___ body **(1)**

10. ev e ___ r ___ y ___ one **(1)**

11. r e ___ a ___ l ___ l ___ y **(1)**

12. m o ___ r ___ ning **(1)**

13. a ___ l ___ so **(1)**

14. a ___ l ___ ways **(1)**

15. f i ___ rst **(1)**

Spelling Words

1. while
2. whole
3. anyway
4. anyone
5. anything
6. favorite
7. once
8. suppose
9. everybody
10. everyone
11. really
12. morning
13. also
14. always
15. first

Study List **On a separate piece of paper, write each Spelling Word. Check your spelling against the words on the list.**

Order of words may vary.

120   Theme 5: **One Land, Many Trails**
Assessment Tip: Total **15** Points

Name _____

Spelling Spree

Contrast Clues The second part of each clue contrasts with the first part. Write a Spelling Word for each clue.

1. not evening, but _____
2. not lots of times, but _____
3. not never, but _____
4. not a fraction, but a _____
5. not a specific thing, but _____
6. not last, but _____

<table>
<tr><td>1. morning (1 point)</td><td>4. whole (1)</td></tr>
<tr><td>2. once (1)</td><td>5. anything (1)</td></tr>
<tr><td>3. always (1)</td><td>6. first (1)</td></tr>
</table>

Hidden Words Write the Spelling Word that is hidden in each row of letters. Don't let the other words fool you!

7. n e v e r y b o d y e s
8. c a t s u p p o s e a t
9. s t o r e a l l y i n g
10. t o w h i l e a r n
11. s i e v e r y o n e a r
12. m a n y w a y a k
13. m e a l s o u n d
14. a l f a l f a v o r i t e n t
15. c a n y o n e e d

h u **m o r n i n g** o a t

7. everybody **(1)**
8. suppose **(1)**
9. really **(1)**
10. while **(1)**
11. everyone **(1)**

12. anyway **(1)**
13. also **(1)**
14. favorite **(1)**
15. anyone **(1)**

Spelling Words

1. while
2. whole
3. anyway
4. anyone
5. anything
6. favorite
7. once
8. suppose
9. everybody
10. everyone
11. really
12. morning
13. also
14. always
15. first

Name _____

Proofreading and Writing

Proofreading Circle the four misspelled Spelling Words in this song. Then write each word correctly.

The sun was burning bright this (mornning)

   while I was working my field alone

I didn't have (anyon) to help me

My (favorit) dog had gone

I (realy) wish I had the money

   to buy my ticket home.

1. while
2. whole
3. anyway
4. anyone
5. anything
6. favorite
7. once
8. suppose
9. everybody
10. everyone
11. really
12. morning
13. also
14. always
15. first

1. morning **(1 point)**

2. anyone **(1)**

3. favorite **(1)**

4. really **(1)**

➤ **Write Tag-Team Poetry** **Pair up with a classmate. Then create a poem about the West by taking turns writing lines. Use Spelling Words from the list.** Responses will vary. **(6)**

Name _____

Starting Anew

Read the paragraph below. Fill in each blank with a word from the box. You will use one word twice.

During the second half of the nineteenth century many
immigrants **(1 point)** _____ from Europe traveled west
across America to begin new lives. Families filed
claims **(1)** _____ on pieces of land. There
they could establish a homestead **(1)** _____ and
raise crops and livestock. Advertisements paid for by the
railroads said that the flat, treeless prairie **(1)** _____
had fertile **(1)** _____ soil for growing crops.
These ads convinced **(1)** _____ many families
that they would have success farming in the region. Some did
succeed, but others became discouraged **(1)** _____
and returned to the East. Many who stayed built homes
from squares of prairie sod **(1)** _____.
With a home built, crops growing, and a healthy
heifer **(1)** _____ grazing in a
fertile **(1)** _____ field nearby,
a family was off to a good start.

Name _____

Pioneer Life

What I **K**now	What I **W**ant to Know	What I **L**earned
Pioneers were people who journeyed to wilderness areas to start farms or ranches. **(2 points)** Pioneer children had to do chores. **(2)**	When did pioneers settle in Nebraska? **(2)** What kinds of work did pioneer children do? **(2)**	The McCance family took a claim in Nebraska in 1885. **(2)** Three-year-olds chased birds out of fields and gathered chips for fuel. Four-year-olds ran errands, took water to field-workers, and gathered eggs. Five-year-olds broke up clods in fields, pulled weeds, fed the cookstove, milked cows, plowed, and herded cows. **(2)**

Assessment Tip: Total **12** Points

Name ____

Across-the-Prairie Crossword

Use these clues to complete the crossword puzzle about *Pioneer Girl*.
(**1 point** for each correct answer)

1 prairie
2 backfire
3 immigrants
4 popcorn
5 calico
6 second
7 dash
8 tallgrass
9 grace
10 seeds
11 herding
12 shortgrass
13 haystack
14 treeless
15 paper

Across

3. Most homesteaders near the McCances were _____.
5. material for making dresses
8. prairie in the wetter eastern part of the Midwest
11. A common job for children was _____ cows.
12. prairie in the dry western part of the Midwest
14. Much of the Great Plains is bare and _____.
15. The McCances' Christmas "tree" was decorated with _____ chains.

Down

1. grassy land
2. When a prairie fire approached, farmers set _____.
4. The McCances used this to decorate their Christmas "tree."
6. The hungry children had to wait for _____ table on holidays.
7. Grace made a mad _____ to escape from the heifer.
9. the real first name of "Pete"
10. Wild geese stole precious _____.
13. The cows made a cave in this.

Assessment Tip: Total **15** Points

Name _____

Join Up!

Read the following fliers, which are modeled on handbills from the 1870s. Use them to answer the questions on page 127.

1

Join the Grange Now!
All Your Neighbors Are!
As a member, you benefit from cooperative prices on farm products and tools. Plus, you can take part in Grange social and educational events.

2

Act Now!
Fight the Big City Bosses!
The railroad bosses say they barely make a profit, but don't you believe it! While we struggle to make ends meet, they are all living lives of luxury in the big cities.

3

Farmers Unite!
It Will Make Your Work Easier!
The Grange is the farmer's friend. It is the one organization created by farmers to improve farmers' lives.

4

Ulysses S. Grant Says,
"Join the Grange!"
Do you listen to your President? You should! President Grant approves of the Grange.

5

Fight the Railroads!
Jefferson and Jackson Would Have!
Rise up, fellow farmers! Join the movement that feeds the great nation of Presidents Thomas Jefferson and Andrew Jackson.

Name _____

Join Up! continued

Answer each question about the fliers on page 126. Then fill in the blanks with the propaganda technique that each flier uses.

Propaganda Techniques

Overgeneralization: making general statements with no basis in fact

Testimonial: using the words of a famous person to support a cause

Bandwagon: persuading people to act because everyone else is

Transfer: associating a famous person with a product or cause

Faulty cause and effect: suggesting that this will make life better

1. How does the first flier persuade farmers to join the Grange?
   by saying that everyone else is **(1 point)**

   Propaganda Technique: Bandwagon **(1)**

2. What does the second flier say about all railroad bosses?
   They are all living lives of luxury in the big cities. **(1)**

   Propaganda Technique: Overgeneralization **(1)**

3. What does the third flier promise?
   that the Grange will make farmers' work easier and improve their

   lives **(1)**

   Propaganda Technique: Faulty cause and effect **(1)**

4. Why does the fourth flier quote President Grant?
   If people like the President, they might do what he says. **(1)**

   Propaganda Technique: Testimonial **(1)**

5. What association does the fifth flier make?
   It associates Presidents Jefferson and Jackson with the Grange

   movement. **(1)**

   Propaganda Technique: Transfer **(1)**

Assessment Tip: Total **10** Points

Name _____

Stress That Syllable!

Read each sentence. Say the underlined word several times, placing stress on a different syllable each time. Circle the choice that shows the correct stress for the underlined word. (The stressed syllable is shown in capital letters.)

1. Grace and Florrie wore dresses made of <u>calico</u>.

   (CAL i co) **(1 point)**   cal I co   cal i CO

2. They sweetened their cereal with <u>molasses</u>.

   MO las ses   (mo LAS ses) **(1)**   mo las SES

3. The family's Christmas tree was <u>decorated</u> with paper chains.

   (DEC o rat ed) **(1)** dec O rat ed   dec o RAT ed   dec o rat ED

4. Spring was their <u>favorite</u> time of year.

   (FA vor ite) **(1)**   fa VOR ite   fa vor ITE

5. Nebraska's <u>population</u> grew rapidly.

   POP u la tion   pop U la tion   (pop u LA tion) **(1)** pop u la TION

6. Poppie was <u>determined</u> to make a success of the farm.

   DE ter mined   (de TER mined) **(1)**   de ter MINED

7. The homesteaders began making <u>preparations</u> for the long winter.

   PREP a ra tions   prep A ra tions   (prep a RA tions) **(1)**   prep a ra TIONS

8. The harsh weather did not <u>discourage</u> them.

   DIS cour age   (dis COUR age) **(1)**   dis cour AGE

Assessment Tip: Total **8** Points

Name _____

Unstressed Syllables

To spell a two-syllable or three-syllable word, divide the word into syllables. Spell the word by syllables, noting carefully the spelling of the unstressed syllable or syllables.

doz | en /dŭz′ ən/   **dis | tance** /dĭs′ təns/

de | stroy /dĭ stroi′/

When you hear the final /ĭj/, /ĭv/, or /ĭs/ sounds, think of these patterns:

/ĭj/ *age* (voy**age**)   /ĭv/ *ive* (nat**ive**)   /ĭs/ *ice* (not**ice**)

► The /ĭj/ sound in *knowledge* is spelled *-edge*, and differs from the usual spelling pattern.

Write each Spelling Word under the heading that shows which syllable is stressed. Underline the unstressed syllable or syllables. Order of answers for each category may vary.

Spelling Words

1. dozen
2. voyage
3. forbid
4. native
5. language
6. destroy
7. notice
8. distance
9. carrot
10. knowledge*
11. captive
12. spinach
13. solid
14. justice
15. ashamed
16. program
17. message
18. respond
19. service
20. relative

First Syllable Stressed

doz<u>en</u> **(1 point)**   capt<u>ive</u> **(1)**

voy<u>age</u> **(1)**   spin<u>ach</u> **(1)**

nat<u>ive</u> **(1)**   sol<u>id</u> **(1)**

lang<u>uage</u> **(1)**   just<u>ice</u> **(1)**

not<u>ice</u> **(1)**   pro<u>gram</u> **(1)**

dis<u>tance</u> **(1)**   mess<u>age</u> **(1)**

car<u>rot</u> **(1)**   serv<u>ice</u> **(1)**

know<u>ledge</u> **(1)**   rel<u>ative</u> **(1)**

Last Syllable Stressed

<u>for</u>bid **(1)**   <u>a</u>shamed **(1)**

<u>de</u>stroy **(1)**   <u>re</u>spond **(1)**

Name _____

Spelling Spree

Write a Spelling Word by combining the beginning of the first word with the ending of the second word.

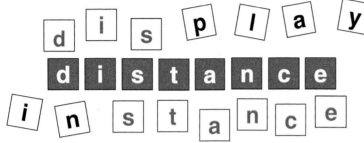

1. capture + olive
2. ashen + framed
3. knowing + pledge
4. nation + forgive
5. languish + passage

6. respect + fond
7. justify + practice
8. serving + office
9. spine + reach
10. progress + madam

1. captive **(1 point)**
2. ashamed **(1)**
3. knowledge **(1)**
4. native **(1)**
5. language **(1)**

6. respond **(1)**
7. justice **(1)**
8. service **(1)**
9. spinach **(1)**
10. program **(1)**

Word Magic Write a Spelling Word to fit each clue.

11. Add two letters to *relate* to write a word for a family member.
12. Replace two letters in *formed* to write a word meaning "to refuse to allow."
13. Insert one consonant into *doze* to write a word meaning "a set of twelve."
14. Replace one letter in *carry* with two to write a word for a root vegetable.
15. Change the ending of *voice* to write a synonym for *journey.*

11. relative **(1)**
12. forbid **(1)**
13. dozen **(1)**
14. carrot **(1)**
15. voyage **(1)**

Spelling Words

1. dozen
2. voyage
3. forbid
4. native
5. language
6. destroy
7. notice
8. distance
9. carrot
10. knowledge*
11. captive
12. spinach
13. solid
14. justice
15. ashamed
16. program
17. message
18. respond
19. service
20. relative

Assessment Tip: Total **15** Points

Name _____

Proofreading and Writing

Proofreading Circle the five misspelled Spelling Words in this journal entry. Then write each word correctly.

Spelling Words

1. dozen
2. voyage
3. forbid
4. native
5. language
6. destroy
7. notice
8. distance
9. carrot
10. knowledge*
11. captive
12. spinach
13. solid
14. justice
15. ashamed
16. program
17. message
18. respond
19. service
20. relative

October 11, 1891

Every day I (notise) something new and different about this strange land, but I still do not know if I will like it here. There is certainly something beautiful about the way the earth and sky stretch into the (distence) as far as the eye can see. At the same time, you live with the knowledge that the land can (distroy) you at any moment. It makes you wish for something more (sollid) than a sod house to call home. The loneliness is hard too. It takes all day just to send a (mesage) to the next farm. I should not complain, though. Our lives are good, and I believe that they will only get better.

1. notice **(1 point)**
2. distance **(1)**
3. destroy **(1)**
4. solid **(1)**
5. message **(1)**

✏ **Write About a Photograph** The photographs used to illustrate the selection show scenes from life on the Great Plains in the 1800s. Choose one that you find interesting. Who are the people in the photograph? What do they seem to be doing? Based on what you read in the selection, what do you think their lives were like?

On a separate piece of paper, write a brief paragraph describing the photograph. Use Spelling Words from the list. Responses will vary. **(5)**

Name _____

Sentences Using Suffixes

Read the dictionary definition for each suffix. Combine each base word in the box with one of the suffixes and write a sentence using the new word. Use each suffix at least once.
Sample answers shown.

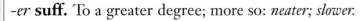

-*er* **suff.** To a greater degree; more so: *neater; slower.*

-*est* **suff.** To the most extreme degree; the most: *greatest; earliest.*

-*ly* **suff.** In a specified manner: *gradually.*

-*ment* **suff.** 1. Act, action, or process. 2. State of being acted upon.

-*ness* **suff.** State, condition, or quality.

Vocabulary

constant
encourage
happy
hard
short
usual

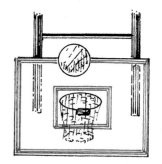

1. I usually shoot baskets in the school gym before I go home. **(2 points)**

2. My older brother needs encouragement to do his homework. **(2)**

3. The little girl is happiest in a room full of puppies. **(2)**

4. I don't like the shortness of winter days. **(2)**

5. Playing chess is harder than it looks. **(2)**

6. My parents are constantly driving me to soccer practice. **(2)**

Assessment Tip: Total **12** Points

Name _____

Possessive Messages

Possessive Pronouns A **possessive pronoun** shows ownership. *My,*
your, his, her, its, our, and *their* appear before nouns that are subjects.
Mine, yours, his, hers, its, ours, and *theirs* stand alone and replace nouns in
sentences.

Possessives Used with Nouns	Possessives That Stand Alone
my This is **my** cup.	**mine** This cup is **mine**.
your **Your** cup is blue.	**yours** **Yours** is blue.
his **His** jacket is torn.	**his** The torn jacket is **his**.
her **Her** dress is new.	**hers** **Hers** is the new dress.
its **Its** food is in the trough.	**its** The food in the trough is **its**.
our Please visit **our** farm.	**ours** The farm is **ours**.
their We walk by **their** fields.	**theirs** Those fields are **theirs**.

**Underline the pronoun in parentheses that correctly completes
each sentence.**

1. (Their/Theirs) favorite place is the meadow. **(1 point)**
2. (My/Mine) is the apple orchard. **(1)**
3. (Our/Ours) is the orchard on Harrow Road. **(1)**
4. What is (your/yours) favorite place? **(1)**
5. Molly's favorite place is (her/hers) room. **(1)**
6. The books are (theirs/their). **(1)**
7. The yellow one is (my/mine). **(1)**
8. (Our/Ours) favorite place is nearby. **(1)**
9. (Her/Hers) is nearby too. **(1)**
10. Where is (your/yours)? **(1)**

Name _____

Contraction Reactions

Contractions with Pronouns A **contraction** is a shortened form of two words. You can combine pronouns with the verbs *am, is, are, will, would, have, has,* and *had* to form **contractions**. Use an apostrophe in place of the dropped letter or letters.

Contractions with Pronouns			
I am	I'm	I have	I've
he is	he's	he has	he's
it is	it's	it has	it's
you are	you're	you have	you've
they are	they're	they have	they've
I will	I'll	I had	I'd
you will	you'll	you had	you'd
we would	we'd	we had	we'd

Rewrite each sentence below, replacing the pronoun and verb with a contraction.

1. It is fun to read about early settlers.

   It's fun to read about early settlers. **(1 point)**

2. I have read two books about pioneer life.

   I've read two books about pioneer life. **(1)**

3. You would like this story about settlers in Oklahoma.

   You'd like this story about settlers in Oklahoma. **(1)**

4. We will visit my grandfather in Oklahoma next summer.

   We'll visit my grandfather in Oklahoma next summer. **(1)**

5. He has lived there all his life.

   He's lived there all his life. **(1)**

Assessment Tip: Total **5** Points

Name _____

It's a Great Invention!

Using *Its* and *It's* A good writer is careful not to confuse the possessive pronoun *its* with the contraction *it's*.

The cat licked **its** paws. **possessive**

It's time for the cat's dinner. **contraction**

Jon wrote this page in his journal. Proofread the copy below and correct the places he has confused the possessive pronoun *its* with the contraction *it's*. Write the correction above each error. (1 point each)

It's   its
~~Its~~ hard to imagine living long ago. Life must have had ~~it'z~~ good

points, but it's hard not to think about what the pioneers didn't have. I

                                                                It's
don't know what I would do without a computer. ~~Its~~ a modern invention

that connects me to the world. The people on the prairie could never

            its
imagine ~~it's~~ usefulness.

It's   it's
~~Its~~ great for doing research. All I have to do is make sure ~~its~~

                        its
plugged in and turn on ~~it's~~ monitor. Then I can find out what pioneer

            It's   it's
life was like. ~~Its~~ not quite the same as living back then, but ~~its~~ the best I

            It's
can do. ~~Its~~ a resource pioneers didn't have. In fact, it's a resource even

my parents didn't have.

Name _____

Writing a Problem-Solution Composition

A **problem-solution composition** outlines a problem and then gives details about the steps leading to its solution.

Prepare to write a problem-solution composition. First, choose one of the topics listed below, or write about how you solved a problem of your own. Then fill in the chart, identifying the problem you will write about, the solution to the problem, details about the steps that led to the solution, and the outcome. The topics are how prairie settlers got water, how they got household supplies, and how they made a holiday festive when money and goods were scarce. Answers will vary.

Problem (2 points)
Solution (2)
Steps toward the solution (2)
Outcome (2)

On a separate sheet of paper, write a two- to three-paragraph problem-solution composition. Begin with an introductory sentence. Then state the problem in the first paragraph. In the following paragraphs, describe the solution to the problem and give details about it. Finally, end with a strong concluding sentence. (4)

Assessment Tip: Total **12** Points

Name _____

Combining Sentences

Good writers streamline their writing by combining short, choppy sentences that have repeated pronouns or nouns into one sentence.

> The prairie **fire** raged all night long. **It** scorched the shortgrass. **It** burned down barns and homes. **It** injured some horses.

> Raging all night long, the prairie fire scorched the shortgrass, burned down barns and homes, and injured some horses.

Read this letter that Grace McCance might have written. Then revise the body of the letter by combining short, choppy sentences that have repeated pronouns or nouns into one sentence. Write the revised letter on the lines. Responses may vary slightly.

Dear Dora,

   How are you? I am still getting used to prairie life. We live in a one-room house made of "Nebraska marble." Poppie made the house himself. He cut blocks of tough prairie earth. He stacked the blocks to construct the walls. He also used a layer of sod for the roof. Our soddy is dark. It is warm in the winter. It is cool in the summer. It is definitely not waterproof, however! Yesterday in a rainstorm, rain leaked right through the roof. Sometimes I really miss Missouri. Write soon!

                                Your friend,

                                Grace

    How are you? I am still getting used to prairie life. We live in a one-room house made of "Nebraska marble." Poppie made the house himself by cutting blocks of tough prairie earth, stacking the blocks to construct the walls, and using a layer of sod for the roof. Our dark soddy is warm in the winter and cool in the summer, but it is definitely not waterproof! Yesterday in a rainstorm, rain leaked right through the roof. Sometimes I really miss Missouri. Write soon! **(10 points)**

Name _____

Tracking Wild Horses

Read the labels below. Write each word from the box under the label that fits it.

Vocabulary

mares	milled	herd
skittered	mustang	remorse
stallion	bluff	ravine

Kinds of Horses

mustang **(1 point)**   stallion **(1)**   mares **(1)**

Landforms

ravine **(1)**   bluff **(1)**

Actions of Horses

milled **(1)**   skittered **(1)**

Feelings

remorse **(1)**

Groups of Animals

herd **(1)**

Use at least three words from the box to write directions for rounding up wild horses.

Answers will vary. **(3)**

_____

_____

_____

Assessment Tip: Total **12** Points

Name _____

Judgments Chart

Sample answers shown.

	Facts from the Selection	Own Values and Experience	Judgment
What kind of person is Bob Lemmons?	He treats his horse very kindly. (**1 point**)	People should be kind to animals. (**1**)	Bob Lemmons does the right thing by treating his horse kindly. (**1**)
What are some of his character traits?	He waits out a rainstorm on the plains. (**1**)	It is uncomfortable to stand outside in a rainstorm. (**1**)	Bob is a physically tough person who is also very patient. (**1**)
What are some more of his character traits?	He spends a whole day standing still and moving slowly to make the herd accept him. (**1**)	It is very hard to stand still for a long time. (**1**)	Bob is patient and has great self-control. (**1**)
What are some of Bob's values?	He lets the rattlesnake live. He says everything in nature has the right to protect itself. (**1**)	Most people who allow creatures to live that can be troublesome have great respect for nature. (**1**)	Bob has great respect for nature. (**1**)
What kind of person is Bob Lemmons?	He doesn't spend any time with the other cowboys. He rides off with his horse and talks to it. (**1**)	People who do not visit with the people they work with may not enjoy the company of other people. (**1**)	He is a loner. He prefers the companionship of his horse to that of people. (**1**)

Name _____

What's So Important About . . . ?

**Tell why each item listed was important in the story of how Bob
Lemmons brought in the herd of wild mustangs.** Sample answers
shown.

1. **tracks in the dirt** Bob read these, realized that a herd of mustangs
   was in the area, and figured out which way they were moving. **(2)**

2. **the lightning** It enabled Bob to see the herd of mustangs across
   the plains. **(2)**

3. **the rainstorm** It washed away the smells of civilization from Bob's
   clothing. **(2)**

4. **the river** Bob knew the wild horses would go there to drink, so he
   he waited nearby. Then, when they came to drink, he acted in a
   way that would make them comfortable with him. **(2)**

5. **the rattlesnake** It bit a colt and the colt died. In the confusion
   that followed, Bob moved to take over the herd. **(2)**

6. **the battle of the stallions** Bob guided Warrior to attack the
   stallion that was the leader of the herd of mustangs. Warrior
   defeated the stallion, enabling Bob to take control of the herd. **(2)**

7. **the corral** Bob led the mustangs back to the corral. When they
   reached the gate, Bob turned Warrior aside while the mustangs
   ran in. **(2)**

140   Theme 5: **One Land, Many Trails**
Assessment Tip: Total **14** Points

Name _____

You Be the Judge

Read the following passage. Then answer the questions on page 142.

Bill Pickett: Master Cowboy

One of the greatest cowboys who ever lived was an African American man named Bill Pickett. He was born in 1870 in west Texas, where he learned to rope and ride early in life. As a young man he worked as a ranch hand and then became a trick rider and rodeo star. He later joined Zack Miller's 101 Ranch Wild West Show—a touring cowboy act—and became the star performer. Miller called him "the greatest sweat and dirt cowhand that ever lived, bar none."

Pickett is credited with inventing the rodeo sport known as bulldogging, also known as steer wrestling. Legend has it that Pickett was herding cattle in 1903, when an ornery steer started tearing around the pasture, scattering the other cattle. Losing his patience, Pickett raced after the steer on his horse, leaped onto its back, and wrestled it to the ground. He later perfected this technique and made bulldogging a regular part of his rodeo act.

One of the most famous incidents involving Pickett occurred in New York's Madison Square Garden. There, Pickett was bulldogging with a young assistant, Will Rogers, who later became a show business star himself. Suddenly, a steer bolted out of the ring and charged into the grandstand. The terrified spectators panicked, but Pickett and Rogers stayed calm. They jumped into the stands and wrestled the giant steer back down to the ring. They not only saved lives that day but also put on a great show!

Theme 5: **One Land, Many Trails**   141

You Be the Judge continued

Answer these questions about the passage on page 141.

1. What judgment about Bill Pickett does the author make in the first paragraph?

   that he was one of the greatest cowboys who ever lived **(1 point)**

2. Do you agree with this judgment? Why or why not?

   Answers will vary. **(1)**

   _____

3. In the rodeo bull wrestling is done purely for sport. Do you think this is right? Give reasons for your judgment.

   Answers will vary. **(2)**

   _____

4. Circle each trait below that you think Bill Pickett possessed. Next to each trait you circle, tell why that trait applies to him.
   Sample answers shown.

Traits	Reasons
(brave)	He did the dangerous work of a cowboy. **(2)**
kind	
(tough)	He wrestled steers for sport. **(2)**
(ambitious)	He went from being a cowhand in west Texas to being a rodeo star. **(2)**

Saddle Up Those Syllables!

Read each sentence. On the line below the sentence, divide the underlined word into syllables, using slashes between the syllables. Then write another sentence using the word. The first one is done for you. Sample sentences shown.

Example: Bob awoke as soon as the sun came over the horizon.

ho/ri/zon On the ocean, nothing blocks a view of the horizon.

1. At daybreak, Bob was immediately awake and ready to ride.

   im/me/di/ate/ly **(1 point)** My dog sits immediately after I give her

   the command. **(2)**

2. Bob Lemmons held his shoulders high as he rode Warrior.

   shoul/ders **(1)** The woman's shoulders ached after an hour of

   shoveling snow. **(2)**

3. A rattlesnake doesn't always give a warning before it strikes.

   rat/tle/snake **(1)** I once read about a rattlesnake with twelve rattles.

   (2)

4. Warrior neighed triumphantly after challenging the stallion.

   tri/um/phant/ly **(1)** The winning swimmer waved triumphantly as

   he accepted his medal. **(2)**

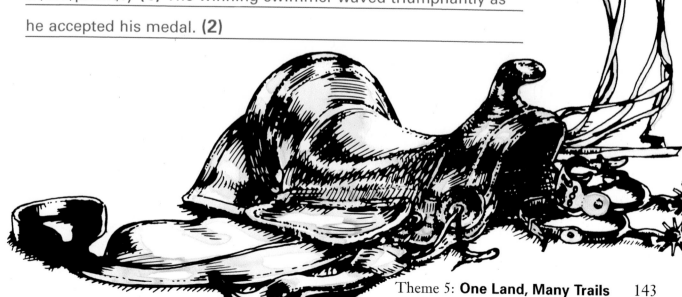

Name _____

Final /n/ or /ən/, /chər/, /zhər/

Each of these words has the final /n/, /ən/, /chər/, or /zhər/ sounds. When you hear these final sounds, think of these patterns:

/n/ or /ən/ *ain* (capt**ain**)   /chər/ *ture* (cul**ture**)

/zhər/ *sure* (trea**sure**)

▶ The /ən/ sound in the starred words *surgeon* and *luncheon* is spelled *eon* and does not follow the usual spelling pattern.

Write each Spelling Word under its final sound.
Order of answers for each category may vary.

1. mountain
2. treasure
3. culture
4. fountain
5. creature
6. captain
7. future
8. adventure
9. moisture
10. surgeon*
11. lecture
12. curtain
13. pasture
14. measure
15. vulture
16. feature
17. furniture
18. pleasure
19. mixture
20. luncheon*

Final /n/ or /ən/ Sound

mountain (**1 point**)   surgeon (**1**)

fountain (**1**)   curtain (**1**)

captain (**1**)   luncheon (**1**)

Final /chər/ Sound

culture (**1**)   pasture (**1**)

creature (**1**)   vulture (**1**)

future (**1**)   feature (**1**)

adventure (**1**)   furniture (**1**)

moisture (**1**)   mixture (**1**)

lecture (**1**)

Final /zhər/ Sound

treasure (**1**)   pleasure (**1**)

measure (**1**)

144   Theme 5: **One Land, Many Trails**
Assessment Tip: Total **20** Points

Name _____

Spelling Spree

Word Root Hunt Write the Spelling Word that has the same root as each word below.

1. pleasing
2. collect
3. furnish
4. capital
5. cultivate
6. surgery
7. pastoral

1. pleasure **(1 point)**
2. lecture **(1)**
3. furniture **(1)**
4. captain **(1)**
5. culture **(1)**
6. surgeon **(1)**
7. pasture **(1)**

Ending Match Write Spelling Words by matching word parts and endings. Be sure to write each ending correctly.

<a> /n/ *or* /ən/   <b> /chər/   <c> /zhər/

8.   vul<b>
9.   fu<b>
10.   trea<c>
11.   curt<a>
12.   mix<b>
13.   mea<c>
14.   lunch<a>
15.   fount<a>

8. vulture **(1)**
9. future **(1)**
10. treasure **(1)**
11. curtain **(1)**
12. mixture **(1)**
13. measure **(1)**
14. luncheon **(1)**
15. fountain **(1)**

Spelling Words

1. mountain
2. treasure
3. culture
4. fountain
5. creature
6. captain
7. future
8. adventure
9. moisture
10. surgeon*
11. lecture
12. curtain
13. pasture
14. measure
15. vulture
16. feature
17. furniture
18. pleasure
19. mixture
20. luncheon*

Theme 5: **One Land, Many Trails**   145
Assessment Tip: Total **15** Points

Name _____

Proofreading and Writing

Proofreading Circle the five misspelled Spelling Words in this travelogue. Then write each word correctly.

The corral sits at the foot of a rise—more than a hill, but not quite a (mountin.) The land doesn't get much (moisure,) and every living (creacher) is always on the lookout for its survival. It is here that Bob Lemmons lives and works. I had the pleasure of meeting Mr. Lemmons shortly after he had captured a herd of mustangs. He has a special way of getting his work done. The most remarkable (featur) of his method is that he gets the horses to accept him as one of them, rather than as a human being. It seemed like quite an (adveture) to me, but to Mr. Lemmons it was all in a day's work.

1. mountain
2. treasure
3. culture
4. fountain
5. creature
6. captain
7. future
8. adventure
9. moisture
10. surgeon*
11. lecture
12. curtain
13. pasture
14. measure
15. vulture
16. feature
17. furniture
18. pleasure
19. mixture
20. luncheon*

1. mountain (**1 point**) 4. feature (**1**)

2. moisture (**1**) 5. adventure (**1**)

3. creature (**1**)

Write a Character Sketch Bob Lemmons was an unusual person who had a very special way of capturing wild mustangs. How would you describe his work? What was his relationship with Warrior like? What were his most outstanding qualities?

On a separate piece of paper, write a character sketch about Bob Lemmons. Use Spelling Words from the list. Responses will vary. **(5)**

Using Parts of Speech

Read the dictionary entries. For each entry word, write two sentences, using the word as a different part of speech in each sentence. Sample answers shown.

clear (klîr) *adj.* Free from clouds, mist, or haze. *v.* To make free of objects or obstructions.

close (klōs) *adj.* Near in space or time. *v.* (klōz) To move so that an opening or a passage is blocked; shut.

faint (fānt) *adj.* Lacking brightness or clarity; dim; indistinct. *v.* To lose consciousness for a short time.

print (prĭnt) *n.* A mark or an impression made in or on a surface by pressure. *v.* To write in block letters.

1. The sky was clear when the plane took off. **(2 points)**

   My chore is to clear the table after dinner. **(2)**

2. The farmhouse was close to the road. **(2)**

   Close the door on your way out! **(2)**

3. The man heard a faint call from the other side of the campground. **(2)**

   If you faint at the sight of blood, you shouldn't become a doctor. **(2)**

4. We knew deer had been in our yard because we saw their prints in the snow. **(2)**

   Please print your name clearly at the top of the page. **(2)**

Name _____

Double Trouble

Double Subjects Do not use a double subject (a noun and a pronoun) to name the same person, place, or thing. Use either the noun or the pronoun as the subject, but not both.

Incorrect:	Lenny he is my brother.
Correct:	Lenny is my brother.
Correct:	He is my brother.

Each sentence below has a double subject. Cross out one unneeded subject, and write your new sentence on the line.

Answers will vary.

1. My aunt and uncle ~~they~~ have a cattle ranch.

   My aunt and uncle have a cattle ranch. **(1 point)**

2. My aunt ~~she~~ runs the business end of things.

   My aunt runs the business end of things. **(1)**

3. ~~The ranch~~ it is big.

   It is big. **(1)**

4. The animals ~~they~~ are taken care of by my uncle.

   The animals are taken care of by my uncle. **(1)**

5. Kurt ~~he~~ is my cousin.

   Kurt is my cousin. **(1)**

6. ~~The horse~~ she trusts Kurt.

   She trusts Kurt. **(1)**

7. Uncle Henry ~~he~~ trains horses.

   Uncle Henry trains horses. **(1)**

8. The stable ~~it~~ is home to six horses.

   The stable is home to six horses. **(1)**

Assessment Tip: Total **8** Points

Name _____

We or Us?

Using *We* and *Us* with Nouns Sometimes a writer may need to use a pronoun before a noun to make clear who is being talked about. Use *we* with a noun subject or after a linking verb. Use *us* with a noun object (a noun that follows an action verb) or after words like *to, for, with, at,* or *in.*

> **subject: We boys** are going to pitch hay.
>
> **object:** The cows will be herded by **us girls.**

Write either *we* or *us* in each blank to correctly complete each sentence.

1. The ranch hands showed __us (1)__ kids how to rope a calf.

2. The best riders were __we (1)__ girls.

3. __We (1)__ cooks made big meals for the ranch hands.

4. It's a great outdoor life for __us (1)__ cowboys.

5. __We (1)__ boys went to the rodeo on Friday.

6. The owners held a square dance for __us (1)__ visitors.

7. __We (1)__ fiddlers need to tune up.

8. The caller shook hands with __us (1)__ greenhorns.

9. __We (1)__ dancers whirled and twirled.

10. Saying good-night was hard for __us (1)__ guests.

Name _____

Who Is He?

Writing Clearly with Pronouns A good writer makes clear
to whom each pronoun refers.

> **Unclear:** After Mel turned hard on the key in the lock, it broke.
>
> **What broke—the key or the lock?**
>
> **Clear:** After Mel turned hard on the key in the lock, the lock broke.
>
> **Clear:** After Mel turned hard on the key in the lock, the key broke.

Shirley wrote the following messages to her friends. Rewrite each sentence with unclear pronoun references to make the references clear.

1. Phil and Bill visited Philadelphia and Pittsburgh. He thinks it has an interesting history.

   Phil (or Bill) thinks Philadelphia (or Pittsburgh) has an interesting

   history. **(2 points)**

2. Julie and Karen joined us in Mississippi. She is my cousin, but I'd never met her before.

   Karen (or Julie) is my cousin, but I'd never met Julie (or Karen)

   before. **(2)**

3. This morning, I fixed breakfast. Then I saw a skunk! The skunk turned around, and I was able to eat it.

   The skunk turned around, and I was able to eat breakfast. **(2)**

   _____

Assessment Tip: Total **6** Points

Name _____

Writing an Explanation

Black Cowboy Wild Horses explains who Bob Lemmons was and how he tracked animals. The purpose of an explanation is to explain one of the following:

► who or what something is

► what is or was important about something or someone

► how something works or worked

► the steps of a process

► why something happens or happened

Prepare to write several paragraphs explaining how Bob Lemmons was able to capture an entire herd of wild horses by himself. To plan and organize your explanation, use the graphic organizer below. First, write the topic in the center box. Then list the steps Lemmons took and details about the process he used. If necessary, look back at the selection to recall how one step led to another.

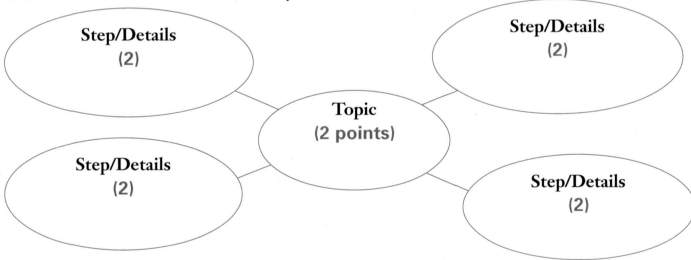

Step/Details (2)

Step/Details (2)

Topic (2 points)

Step/Details (2)

Step/Details (2)

On a separate sheet of paper, write a two- to three-paragraph explanation, using the information you recorded. In the first sentence or paragraph, clearly state the topic. Then present the steps in a logical order, providing enough steps and clarifying details to help readers understand how this event happened. Be sure to define any special or technical terms the first time you use them. Finally, end with a conclusion. (5)

Name _____

Black Cowboy Wild Horses

Writing Skill Improving Your Writing

Organizing Information

A good writer organizes ideas in a logical way so that readers understand his or her writing. You can organize ideas in your own writing by sequence of events, by causes and effects, or by main ideas and details.

This explanation by an animal tracker like Bob Lemmons has been scrambled. Put the sentences in an order that makes sense. Then rewrite the explanation on the lines.

How to "Read" Animal Tracks

One way to locate an animal is by finding and studying its tracks. Once you identify what animal left a particular track, you can determine how long ago it passed by. To find tracks, try starting near water. A fresh, soft, sharply outlined track means an animal was recently in the area, but a hard, dry, less clearly defined track indicates that time has passed since the animal was there. After you've discovered a set of tracks, you can study their shape and size to figure out what kind of animal made them. Animals often leave tracks on the muddy banks of streams and ponds where they come to drink or hunt food.

One way to locate an animal is by finding and studying its tracks. To find tracks, try starting near water. Animals often leave tracks on the muddy banks of streams and ponds where they come to drink or hunt food. After you've discovered a set of tracks, you can study their shape and size to figure out what kind of animal made them. Once you identify what animal left a particular track, you can determine how long ago it passed by. A fresh, soft, sharply outlined track means an animal was recently in the area, but a hard, dry, less clearly defined track indicates that time has passed since the animal was there. **(12 points)**

152   Theme 5: **One Land, Many Trails**
Assessment Tip: Total **12** Points

Name _____

Ride Those Riddles

Write a word from the box to answer each riddle.

1. Which word names a type of hat?
   sombrero **(1 point)**

2. Which word names injuries?
   wounds **(1)**

3. Which word means "completely changed"?
   transformed **(1)**

4. Which word describes someone who is well known for
   something bad? notorious **(1)**

5. Which word describes something rough, difficult, or
   uneven? rugged **(1)**

6. Which word means "expressions of sympathy"?
   condolences **(1)**

7. Which word means "without delay"?
   urgently **(1)**

8. Which word names a kind of ruler?
   dictator **(1)**

Vocabulary

rugged
wounds
sombrero
urgently
notorious
condolences
dictator
transformed

Theme 5: **One Land, Many Trails**   153
Assessment Tip: Total **8** Points

Story Map

Sample answers shown.

Characters	
The family: Elena, Pablo, and their children: Rosa, the narrator, Luis, Esteban, and María **(1)**	**Other Characters:** the villagers, Pancho Villa and his followers, the Chinese fruit seller **(1)**

Setting	
Where the story takes place: rural Mexico; Ciudad Juárez; Santa Ana, California **(1)**	**When the story takes place:** in the early 1900s beginning in 1910 **(1)**

Plot

Problem: Pablo dies in a riding accident just as the Mexican Revolution is beginning. Elena and the children must leave. **(1)**

Events:

1. At first Elena is crazy with grief but then grows quiet. **(1)**

2. One day Pancho Villa and his men arrive in the village, and Elena hides her eldest son and the horses in the kitchen. **(1)**

3. Elena gives Villa the last hat, and he has his men protect the house. **(1)**

4. Elena gathers money, clothing, and food, and takes her children on the train to Ciudad Juárez. **(1)**

5. Elena befriends a Chinese fruit seller who helps her get Esteban across the border. **(1)**

6. The family goes from San Francisco to Los Angeles, before settling in Santa Ana, where Elena runs a boardinghouse. The children also go to school, where they learn to be "real" Americans. **(1)**

Resolution: The children learn that their village in Mexico had been burned to the ground and many people had died during the war. **(1)**

Assessment Tip: Total **12** Points

Name _____

A Portrait of Elena

Complete the sentences below to show how Elena's feelings and character traits are revealed through her actions. The first sentence has been completed for you. Sample answers shown.

In Mexico, in the family's home village	On the way to the United States	In California
Example: Elena shows her **deep love for her husband** when she strokes his hand and speaks gently to him while he is dying.	In the plaza, just before leaving the village, Elena shows **generosity** when she gives away all the goods from her shop. **(2)**	Elena shows she is **hard-working** when she runs a boarding-house to support her family. **(2)**
Elena shows **her grief** when she weeps, knocks down her flowerpots, and lets her pet birds go. **(2 points)**	In Ciudad Juárez, Elena shows **love for her son** Esteban when she figures out a way to get him across the border. **(2)**	Elena shows that she **values education** when she tells the children that school and home-work come first. **(2)**
Elena shows **cleverness** when she hides Esteban and the horses in the kitchen. **(2)**		Elena shows she **wants her children to grow up "strong and full of hope"** when she does not tell them that their village in Mexico had been burned to the ground. **(2)**
Elena shows **courage** when she opens the door for Pancho Villa. **(2)**		

Assessment Tip: Total **16** Points

Name _____

Mapping the Story

Read the passage. Then complete the activity on page 157.

A Dangerous Journey

My grandfather began his life in 1898 in the Italian village of Corato, in southern Italy. In such villages, people of all ages were occupied with growing food and tending animals. Life responded to the rhythm of the seasons. As a boy, my grandfather cared for the local horses and worked in the fields as a farmhand.

By the time my grandfather was in his teens, World War I had broken out in Europe. One by one, the countries surrounding Italy entered the war. Italy managed to stay out of the fighting for nearly a year, but it was clearly only a matter of time before Italy, too, would be drawn into the conflict.

A powerful farm boy, my grandfather was a prime candidate for the Italian army. His mother, my great-grandmother, did not want to lose her son to war. She made what must have been one of the most difficult decisions of her life: she decided to send her son far away to America.

At that time, young men were being rounded up and forced to join the Italian army. My grandfather's family faced a daunting task—how to send my grandfather across Italy and onto a boat bound for America without the authorities finding out.

Very early one morning, well before dawn, a horse-drawn cart pulled up to my grandfather's house. The cart was filled with hay. To a casual observer, the cart was simply on its way from one farm to the next to deliver a load of hay. When the cart pulled away from the house, however, my grandfather lay hidden beneath the hay. In one hand he held a bundle that contained all his belongings. In the other, he held bread, fruit, and meat—enough food, his mother hoped, to last for at least part of the long journey that lay ahead.

The cart was bound for Bari, a seaport town on Italy's east coast. There my grandfather's family had arranged for a boat to take him on the first leg of the journey to America.

Name _____

Mapping the Story continued

Answer these questions about the passage on page 156.

1. What is the setting in which the events described in the passage take place? (Include both the time and place.)
   Italy at the beginning of World War I **(2 points)**
   _____

2. Who are the main characters in the passage?
   the narrator's grandfather and great-grandmother **(2)**
   _____

3. What problem is described in the passage?
   The narrator's grandfather must find a way to escape from Italy
   before he is forced to join the army. **(3)**
   _____

4. What is the solution to this problem?
   His family sneaks him out of the village in a cart full of hay, which
   takes him to Bari, a port town. There a boat will take him to
   America. **(4)**
   _____

5. Use the information above to write a brief summary of the passage.
   The narrator's grandfather was born in an Italian village in 1898.
   When he was a teenager, World War I broke out in Europe.
   Although Italy did not enter the war right away, it was only a
   matter of time before it would become involved. The narrator's
   grandfather's family did not want him to be forced to join the
   Italian army, so they hid him in a hay wagon and arranged for him
   to travel by boat to America. **(4)**

Name _____

I Spy the *Y*

Read the letter that Rosa might have written to a friend in Mexico. Circle words in which a *y* changed to *i* before an ending or suffix was added. On the lines below the letter, write the base word and the ending or suffix for each circled word.

Dear Maria,

　　I wish you could see California. It is (beautiful!) I will always love Mexico too, but I like it even better here. We live in the (loveliest) valley! And just think—there are no (flies!) We are so much (luckier) than the many (families) who were not able to escape the war in Mexico. I know Mother (worried) about how she could make a life for us here. But she has a good job, and we know the future is bright for all of us.

　　　　　　　　Love,

　　　　　　　　Rosa

(1 point for each circled word)

1. beauty **(1 point)** + -ful **(1)**
2. lovely **(1)** + -est **(1)**
3. fly **(1)** + -es **(1)**
4. lucky **(1)** + -er **(1)**
5. family **(1)** + -es **(1)**
6. worry **(1)** + -ed **(1)**

Assessment Tip: Total **18** Points

Name _____

Changing Final *y* to *i*

Each Spelling Word has an ending or a suffix added to a base word. When a word ends with a consonant and *y*, change the *y* to *i* when adding -*es*, -*ed*, -*er*, -*est*, or -*ness*.

army + es = arm**ies**   spy + ed = sp**ied**

dirty + er = dirt**ier**   scary + est = scar**iest**

happy + ness = happ**iness**

Write each Spelling Word. Underline the letter that replaced the final *y* when the ending or the suffix was added.

Order of responses may vary.

Spelling Words

1. liberties
2. victories
3. countries
4. spied
5. enemies
6. armies
7. scariest
8. dirtier
9. happiness
10. abilities
11. pitied
12. ladies
13. busier
14. duties
15. lilies
16. worthiness
17. tiniest
18. emptiness
19. replies
20. dizziness

Final *y* changed to *i*

liber<u>t</u>ies **(1 point)**   pit<u>i</u>ed **(1)**

victor<u>i</u>es **(1)**   lad<u>i</u>es **(1)**

countr<u>i</u>es **(1)**   bus<u>i</u>er **(1)**

sp<u>i</u>ed **(1)**   dut<u>i</u>es **(1)**

enem<u>i</u>es **(1)**   lil<u>i</u>es **(1)**

arm<u>i</u>es **(1)**   worth<u>i</u>ness **(1)**

scar<u>i</u>est **(1)**   tin<u>i</u>est **(1)**

dirt<u>i</u>er **(1)**   empt<u>i</u>ness **(1)**

happ<u>i</u>ness **(1)**   repl<u>i</u>es **(1)**

abilit<u>i</u>es **(1)**   dizz<u>i</u>ness **(1)**

Name _____

Spelling Spree

Adding Suffixes Write a Spelling Word by adding the
correct suffix to the word part in each phrase below.

1. a trip through seven countr_____
2. dirt_____ than a pigsty
3. the dut_____ of the president
4. lad_____ and gentlemen
5. the empt_____ of a beach in winter
6. to send repl_____ to letters
7. a beautiful bouquet of lil_____

1. countries **(1 point)**
2. dirtier **(1)**
3. duties **(1)**
4. ladies **(1)**
5. emptiness **(1)**
6. replies **(1)**
7. lilies **(1)**

Word Clues Write a Spelling Word to fit each clue.

8. another word for *freedoms*
9. having more work to do
   than another
10. watched sneakily
11. felt sorry for
12. a synonym for *joy*
13. the most frightening
    of all
14. the opposite of *friends*
15. a result of spinning
    around

8. liberties **(1)**
9. busier **(1)**
10. spied **(1)**
11. pitied **(1)**
12. happiness **(1)**
13. scariest **(1)**
14. enemies **(1)**
15. dizziness **(1)**

Assessment Tip: Total **15** Points

Name _____

Proofreading and Writing

Proofreading **Circle the five misspelled Spelling Words in this newspaper article. Then write each word correctly.**

Guadalajara—The situation in Mexico continues to grow more serious. The government has no control over large areas of the country, and the rebel armys are increasing in strength. Each one of their victaries brings more support to the revolution. It is feared that by 1911 Mexico will be in even worse shape.

The rebels are hoping that the leaders of foreign countries will see the worthyness of their cause and send aid. Even the tieniest amount, they say, would be a great help. In the meantime, the Mexican people continue to suffer, while caring for their families to the best of their ablities.

Spelling Words

1. liberties
2. victories
3. countries
4. spied
5. enemies
6. armies
7. scariest
8. dirtier
9. happiness
10. abilities
11. pitied
12. ladies
13. busier
14. duties
15. lilies
16. worthiness
17. tiniest
18. emptiness
19. replies
20. dizziness

1. armies **(1 point)**   4. tiniest **(1)**

2. victories **(1)**   5. abilities **(1)**

3. worthiness **(1)**

- **Write a Screenplay** Suppose that *Elena* was being made into a movie. Think about the scene between Elena and Pablo just before Pablo dies. What do the characters say to each other during this scene? Are they sitting or standing while they talk? What tone of voice do they use? Do they look at each other while speaking?

On a separate piece of paper, write a screenplay for the scene between Elena and Pablo. Be sure to indicate when each new speaker begins. Use Spelling Words from the list. Responses will vary. **(5)**

Name _____

Using Word Histories

Read the dictionary entries. Then read the sentences. For each underlined word, write the word origin and its meaning. Then use the clues to think of other common English words that have the same origin.

conquer 1. To defeat or subdue by force. 2. To gain control by overcoming difficulties. [Latin *com-*, intensive prefix + *quaerere*, to seek.]

expect To look forward to the probable occurrence or appearance of. [Latin *ex-*, off, away + *spectāre*, to look at.]

memory 1. The power or ability of remembering past experiences. 2. Something remembered. [Latin *memoria*, memory.]

1. Rosa had only a faint <u>memory</u> of her father.

   Word root: _memoria **(1 point)**_

   Meaning: _memory **(1)**_

   a monument or holiday that serves as a remembrance of a person or

   event _memorial **(1)**_

   to commit to memory; learn by heart _memorize **(1)**_

2. Elena did not <u>expect</u> that Pancho Villa would ask for a sombrero.

   Word root: _spectāre **(1)**_

   Meaning: _to look at **(1)**_

   an observer of an event _spectator **(1)**_

   a pair of eyeglasses _spectacles **(1)**_

3. Elena had <u>conquered</u> mathematics and valued education.

   Word root: _quaerere **(1)**_

   Meaning: _to seek **(1)**_

   to request information by asking questions _inquire **(1)**_

   to get; gain; obtain _acquire **(1)**_

Assessment Tip: Total **12** Points

Name _____

How? When? Where?

Adverbs An adverb tells *how*, *when*, or *where*. Adverbs can describe verbs. Many adverbs end in *-ly*.

How	When	Where
fast	tomorrow	here
hard	later	inside
happily	again	north
quietly	first	forward
slowly	then	upstairs

Underline the adverb in each sentence below. Then on the line write *how*, *when*, or *where* to show what the adverb tells.

1. Elena and her family quickly left their home. _how **(1 point)**_

2. They left early in the morning. _when **(1)**_

3. The family traveled north. _where **(1)**_

4. Everyone worked hard. _how **(1)**_

5. The children greatly admired their mother. _how **(1)**_

6. Did you suddenly leave? _when **(1)**_

7. I stepped carefully over the ice. _how **(1)**_

8. She went inside. _where **(1)**_

9. Look closely at this picture. _how **(1)**_

10. Do you see now? _when **(1)**_

Prepare to Compare

Comparing with Adverbs To compare two actions, add *-er* to most one-syllable adverbs; use *more* with adverbs of two or more syllables. To compare three or more actions, add *-est* to most one-syllable adverbs; use *most* with adverbs of two or more syllables.

My little sister runs **fast**.　　　　The weather here changes **quickly**.

My brother runs **faster** than she does.　It changes **more quickly** at the shore.

My big sister runs **fastest** of all.　　It changes **most quickly** in the mountains.

Write the correct form of the adverb to complete each sentence.

1. My alarm clock rings early.

2. My dad's alarm rings <u>earlier **(1 point)**</u> than mine.

3. My brother's alarm rings <u>earliest **(1)**</u> of all.

4. The retriever barks excitedly.

5. Our German shepherd barks <u>more excitedly **(1)**</u>.

6. Of all the dogs, however, the chihuahua barks
<u>most excitedly **(1)**</u>.

7. Kim studies hard every evening.

8. Juan studies <u>harder **(1)**</u> than Kim.

9. Sonya studies <u>hardest **(1)**</u> of all.

10. Jim scored high on the test.

11. His brother scored <u>higher **(1)**</u> than Jim.

12. Of everyone in the class, Celia scored
the <u>highest **(1)**</u>.

13. I painted carefully.

14. Mom painted <u>more carefully **(1)**</u> than I did.

15. Dad painted the <u>most carefully **(1)**</u> of all!

Assessment Tip: Total **10** Points

Name _____

Expand Your Description

Expanding Sentences with Adverbs A good writer expands sentences with adverbs to describe action more clearly.

Camille bakes bread.   Camille **cheerfully** bakes bread.

Anna wants her pen-pal in Mexico to imagine what life is like in her house, but she has not used any adverbs. On a separate sheet of paper rewrite her letter, adding adverbs from the list or those of your own choosing.

slightly
suddenly
excitedly
noisily
happily
loudly
gracefully
still
carefully
peacefully
immediately
heartily

Hi Pen-pal!
My family's dinner last night was unusual. We celebrated my good report card with a special dinner. Here is what happened: We all pulled out our chairs. My brother Todd remembered that the cat Clive was outside. Todd jumped up, and his chair fell to the floor. Everyone laughed. Mom carved the roast. Without warning, Clive lept into the middle of the table. Todd decided to put him back outside. We ate the rest of our dinner.

Your friend,
Anna

Sample answer: My family's dinner last night was <u>slightly</u> unusual. We <u>happily</u> celebrated my good report card with a special dinner. Here is what happened: We all <u>noisily</u> pulled out our chairs. My brother Todd <u>suddenly</u> remembered that the cat Clive was <u>still</u> outside. Todd jumped up <u>excitedly</u>, and his chair fell <u>loudly</u> to the floor. Everyone laughed <u>heartily</u>. Mom <u>carefully</u> carved the roast. Without warning, Clive <u>gracefully</u> lept into the middle of the table. Todd <u>immediately</u> decided to put him back outside. We <u>peacefully</u> ate the rest of our dinner.
(10 points)

Name _____

Writing a Compare/ Contrast Paragraph

In *Elena*, you read about how the lives of Elena and her children changed as a result of the Mexican Revolution in the early 1900s. One way to explore how things are alike and different is by writing a **compare/contrast paragraph.** Comparing shows how things are alike, and contrasting shows how they are different. A good compare/contrast paragraph describes both the ways things are alike and the ways they are different.

Use this Venn diagram to help you gather details about Elena's family's life in Mexico and about their life later in the United States.

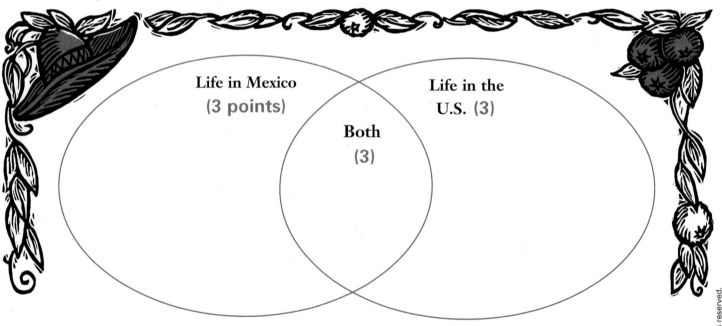

Life in Mexico
(3 points)

Both
(3)

Life in the
U.S. (3)

On a separate sheet of paper, write a paragraph in which you use details from your Venn diagram to compare and contrast Elena's family's life in rural Mexico with their life in Santa Ana, California. In the opening sentence, clearly state the subject being compared and contrasted. In the supporting sentences, group details that compare and details that contrast in a clear manner. (6)

Assessment Tip: Total **15** Points

Name _____

Using Exact Adverbs

Adverbs such as *suddenly* and *wildly* clarify and enhance verbs or adjectives. A good writer uses exact adverbs to help sharpen the differences and similarities between things and to make details more vivid.

Suppose that Pablo made an advertisement for his sombreros. Read the ad and replace the inexact adverbs that have been underlined with more exact adverbs from the list. Write your revised ad on the lines. (2 points each)

Adverbs

richly

drably

supremely

handsomely

exceptionally

exquisitely

Why dress plainly when you can dress well instead? Buy a very well-made sombrero by Pablo. Unlike other hat makers, Pablo fashions his famous hats with velvety soft, smooth felt and then trims them nicely with gleaming silver. From the shaped crown to the detailed brim, Pablo's hats are certainly crafted. Pancho Villa says, "I'd never wear another. Pablo's sombreros are the finest in all of Mexico." You will be very happy wearing a one-of-a-kind sombrero by Pablo!

Why dress **drably** when you can dress **handsomely** instead? Buy an

exceptionally well-made sombrero by Pablo. Unlike other hat makers,

Pablo fashions his famous hats with velvety soft, smooth felt and then

trims them **richly** with gleaming silver. From the shaped crown to the

detailed brim, Pablo's hats are **exquisitely** crafted. Pancho Villa says, "I'd

never wear another. Pablo's sombreros are the finest in all of Mexico." You

will be **supremely** happy wearing a one-of-a-kind sombrero by Pablo!

Name _____

Bridge Puzzle

Fill each blank with a Vocabulary word. Then follow the directions below.

Vocabulary

bustle   turnpike
luxury   wondrous
omen

1. If you want something expensive that you don't really need, you want a (l) u x u r y. **(2 points)**

2. If you want to travel on a fast road, and you don't mind paying a toll, you should drive on the t u r n p i (k) (e). **(2)**

3. If you are amazed, you may have just seen something w (o) (n) d (r) o u s. **(2)**

4. If you want some peace and quiet, you need to stay away from b u s (t) l e. **(2)**

5. If something predicts good luck for the future, it is a good o m e (n). **(2)**

Cayuga Bridge was the longest bridge in the United States in Mem Nye's time. What is the country's longest bridge today? Use the letters you circled to fill in the blanks below. Write the letters in the order you circled them.

The L A K E P O N T C H A R T R A I N Causeway in

Louisiana is almost 24 miles long. **(2 points** for completing puzzle**)**

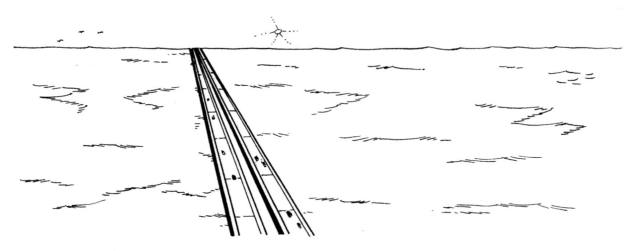

Assessment Tip: Total **12** Points

Name _____

Making Judgments

As you read each selection, fill the chart below to make judgments about the main characters. Answers will vary. Accept reasonable responses.

	Facts from the Selection	Judgment
Does Mem Nye have a good attitude about traveling to her new home?	1. **(1 point** for each fact**)** 2. **(1)** 3. **(1)**	**(2)**
Does Robert Farnsworth do a good job of adapting to his new home?	1. **(1)** 2. **(1)** 3. **(1)**	**(2)**

Name _____

Conclusions Chart

Use the chart to draw conclusions about Mem's feelings about her brother in *Journey to Nowhere*. Then complete the chart by drawing conclusions about Rosa's feelings about her mother in *Elena*.

Answers may vary. Sample answers are given.

	Story Clues		Conclusions
Journey to Nowhere: What are Mem's feelings about her brother?	She runs all the way down to the bridge with him; she tells him to wait for their parents to cross the bridge; she says she won't fish him out. **(2 points)**	**+** She notices that Joshua chooses the same candy she does, eats it right away, and makes a mess. **(2)**	**=** Mem sometimes thinks her brother is immature, but she also has fun with him. **(2)**
Elena: What are Rosa's feelings about her mother?	She says her mother has great courage and determination; she says her mother saved the family. **(2)**	**+** She tells how hard her mother works; she talks about the wonderful stories her mother tells of the old days. **(2)**	**=** Rosa admires her mother's bravery and hard work; she also thinks her mother is an interesting person. **(2)**

Assessment Tip: Total **12** Points

Klondike Words

Complete each statement with a word from the box.

1. When a small village grows very quickly, it becomes a <u>boomtown **(2 points)**</u>.

2. If your time in the army is over, you have finished your <u>tour of duty **(2)**</u>.

3. If you want to keep something in good shape, you want to <u>maintain **(2)**</u> it.

4. Soldiers live in <u>barracks **(2)**</u>.

5. If you want to study real examples of something, you need <u>specimens **(2)**</u>.

6. You might see deer, elk, and <u>caribou **(2)**</u> in Alaska's wide open spaces.

Name _____

Test Practice

Use the three steps you've learned to write an answer to these questions about *Robert Farnsworth: Army Post on the Yukon*. Make a chart on a separate piece of paper and then write your answer on the lines below. Use the checklist to revise your answer.

1. Why do you think Robert Farnsworth and his family were sad to leave Alaska? Use details from the selection in your response.

   To score each student's answer, use the Checklist

   for Writing an Answer to a Question.

   _____

   _____

   _____

   _____

   _____

   _____

   _____

   _____

   _____

   _____

   _____

Checklist for Writing an Answer to a Question

✔ Did I restate the question at the beginning? (**2 points**)

✔ Can I add more details from what I read to support my answer? (5)

✔ Do I need to delete details that do not help answer the question? (2)

✔ Where can I add more exact words? (2)

✔ Did I write carefully, using clear handwriting? (2)

✔ Did I make mistakes in grammar, spelling, or usage? (2)

Continue on page 173.

Name _____

Test Practice continued

2. **Connecting/Comparing** Compare the attitudes of Robert Farnsworth in *Robert Farnsworth: Army Post on the Yukon* and Joshua Nye in *Journey to Nowhere* toward their new surroundings. Use details from both selections in your answers.

_____ To score each student's answer, use the Checklist _____

_____ for Writing an Answer to a Question. _____

_____

_____

_____

_____

_____

_____

_____

_____

_____

_____

_____

Checklist for Writing an Answer to a Question

✔ Did I restate the question at the beginning? **(2 points)**

✔ Can I add more details from what I read to support my answer? **(5)**

✔ Do I need to delete details that do not help answer the question? **(2)**

✔ Where can I add more exact words? **(2)**

✔ Did I write carefully, using clear handwriting? **(2)**

✔ Did I make mistakes in grammar, spelling, or usage? **(2)**

Read your answers to Questions 1 and 2 aloud to a partner. Then discuss the questions on the checklist. Make any changes that will improve your answers.

Assessment Tip: Total **30** Points

Identify Propaganda

Read each statement below. Decide if it is propaganda and why. Decide which technique each statement uses, if any.

COME TO CALIFORNIA Where the ground is made of GOLD

Propaganda Techniques

Overgeneralization: making general statements based on few or no facts

Testimonial: using a celebrity or an expert to support a product

Bandwagon: persuading consumers to do something because "everyone else" is doing it

Flattery: making people feel "smart" for using a product or doing something

Transfer: causing consumers to transfer their admiration for a person to a product

Faulty cause and effect: promising benefits for consumers if they use a product

1. "Canandaigua General Store: We Have Everything Smart Folks Need!"

   Is this propaganda? <u>yes</u>   Why? <u>The claim to have "everything"</u>
   <u>cannot possibly be factual, and it calls its customers smart.</u>

   Propaganda Technique(s): <u>overgeneralization, flattery</u> **(5 points)**

2. "Lake Ontario General Supply: Let Us Outfit You for the Frontier!"

   Is this propaganda? <u>no</u>   Why? <u>This ad is not propaganda; the</u>
   <u>ad doesn't rely on any of the propaganda techniques.</u>

   Propaganda Technique(s): <u>none</u> **(5)**

3. "Hank's Feed Store: Your Horses Will Love Our Hay!"

   Is this propaganda? <u>yes</u>   Why? <u>It promises something that</u>
   <u>may not happen as a result of buying hay.</u>

   Propaganda Technique(s): <u>faulty cause and effect</u> **(5)**

4. "Sheriff Dan Coe says: 'I read The Gazette! So do your neighbors!'"

   Is this propaganda? <u>yes</u>   Why? <u>It uses the sheriff, a celebrity,</u>
   <u>to advertise and claims that everyone else is reading The Gazette.</u>

   Propaganda Technique(s): <u>testimonial, bandwagon</u> **(5)**

Assessment Tip: Total **20** Points

In My Judgment...

Read the questions and information. Review *Journey to Nowhere* **on Anthology pages 570B–570G for details about Joshua. Then complete the chart to make your character judgments about Joshua.** Sample answers appear in the chart.

	Facts/Clues from the Selection	Own Values and Experience	Judgment
What kind of person is Joshua?	Joshua got excited and ran to the bridge. He darted back and forth on the bridge.	Little kids like to run around; it's hard for them to be still. **(1 point)**	I think Joshua is like most boys, very active. **(1)**
What are Joshua's character traits?	He is young, wants to hurry, gets excited, and runs faster than his feet can go. He doesn't wait to eat his peppermint.	Younger children don't like to wait for things; I get excited and like to explore when I'm on a new adventure. **(1)**	I think Joshua is a very curious person who can't wait to explore new things. He's also impatient. **(1)**
What things does Joshua value in life?	He wants to hurry to see the bridge up close. He wants to cross the bridge right away.	When I hurry to do something new, it's usually because I'm excited about it. **(1)**	I think Josh values being free to explore and experience all kinds of things. **(1)**
Will Joshua have any problems at the family's new home?	He likes every new thing the family comes across. He is excited to cross the bridge.	At first, I might not like moving to a new place, but later I might like it. **(1)**	I think he will do fine, but he might get in trouble because he is so curious and impatient. **(1)**

Theme 5: **One Land, Many Trails**   175

Assessment Tip: Total **8** Points

Changing back to *y*

Read the sentences. Underline the word in each sentence that has one of these endings: *-es, -ed, -er, -est, -ness.* Then write the final *y* base word for the word you underlined.

1. The Old West theater had several <u>balconies</u> with fancy seats.
   balcony **(2 points)**

2. The <u>frostiness</u> of the window let us know how cold it was.
   frosty **(2)**

3. Elena was able to get <u>married</u> to Pablo after her parents gave up their

   objections. marry **(2)**

4. The shrewd ranch owner was one of the <u>canniest</u> businessmen in the

   area. canny **(2)**

5. Her older, know-it-all sister was <u>bossier</u> than her other sister.
   bossy **(2)**

Assessment Tip: Total **10** Points

Name _____

Making Analogies

Read each analogy sentence. Complete each analogy by writing the correct word. After each sentence, write a letter from the key below that describes the relationship between each pair of words.

O = opposites

S = synonyms or near-synonyms

C = example of a category

P = a part of a whole

1. *Acres* are to *land* as *bushels* are to <u>apples, P **(2 points)**</u>.
   farm   *apples*   *oceans*

2. *Silk* is to *cloth* as *sock* is to <u>clothes, C **(2)**</u>.
   dress   *shoes*   *clothes*

3. *Calf* is to *cow* as *chick* is to <u>hen, C **(2)**</u>.
   egg   *hen*   *bunny*

4. *Homesteader* is to *settler* as *bandit* is to <u>outlaw, S **(2)**</u>.
   cowboy   *soldier*   *outlaw*

5. *Courageous* is to *cowardly* as *wise* is to <u>foolish, O **(2)**</u>.
   foolish   *unwitting*   *smart*

6. *Saddle* is to *horse* as *seat* is to <u>wagon, C **(2)**</u>.
   bridle   *buffalo*   *wagon*

Name _____

Spelling Review

Write Spelling Words from the list on this page to answer the questions. Order of answers in each category may vary.

1.–8. Which eight words have the prefix *un-*, *dis-*, *in-*, or *re-*, or the suffix *-ion*?

1. promotion **(1 point)**

2. unable **(1)**

3. tension **(1)**

4. discover **(1)**

5. react **(1)**

6. inspect **(1)**

7. correction **(1)**

8. respond **(1)**

9.–15. Which seven words have the final /n/, /ən/, /chər/, or /zhər/ sounds?

9. treasure **(1)**

10. vulture **(1)**

11. curtain **(1)**

12. furniture **(1)**

13. mountain **(1)**

14. pleasure **(1)**

15. adventure **(1)**

16.–22. In which seven words was the final *y* changed to *i* before an ending was added?

16. pitied **(1)**

17. countries **(1)**

18. spied **(1)**

19. happiness **(1)**

20. dirtier **(1)**

21. scariest **(1)**

22. busier **(1)**

23.–30. Which nine words are partly spelled below? Write each word. Then draw a line to divide each word into syllables.

23. sol— sol | id **(2)**

24. —age voy | age **(2)**

25. spin— spin | ach **(2)**

26. no— no | tice **(2)**

27. —tance dis | tance **(2)**

28. de— de | stroy **(2)**

29. lan— lan | guage **(2)**

30. —tive na | tive **(2)**

Spelling Words

adventure
treasure
solid
promotion
vulture
busier
voyage
unable
spinach
tension
curtain
pitied
furniture
notice
discover
react
mountain
countries
pleasure
spied
happiness
inspect
distance
correction
destroy
dirtier
language
native
respond
scariest

Assessment Tip: Total **38** Points

Name _____

Spelling Spree

Sentence Fillers **Write the Spelling Word that best completes each sentence.**

1. A person born in France is a <u>native **(1 point)**</u> of France.

2. People in France speak the French <u>language **(1)**</u>.

3. We did not mean to <u>destroy **(1)**</u> your flowers.

4. There was great <u>tension **(1)**</u> between the two rivals.

5. A pirate buried his <u>treasure **(1)**</u> in the sand.

6. Mom's <u>promotion **(1)**</u> at work makes her a manager.

7. A cruise is a long sea <u>voyage **(1)**</u>.

8. Lower the <u>curtain **(1)**</u> when the play is over.

9. You might see snow on a <u>mountain **(1)**</u> peak.

10. Eating <u>spinach **(1)**</u> will give you strong bones.

Spelling Words

language
mountain
spinach
voyage
curtain
treasure
native
furniture
discover
promotion
destroy
tension
dirtier
happiness
pleasure

Word Hunt **Each word below is hidden in a Spelling Word. Write the Spelling Word.**

11. cove <u>discover **(1)**</u>

12. tier <u>dirtier **(1)**</u>

13. pine <u>happiness **(1)**</u>

14. plea <u>pleasure **(1)**</u>

15. urn <u>furniture **(1)**</u>

Name _____

Proofreading and Writing

Proofreading Circle the six misspelled Spelling Words in this letter. Then write each word correctly.

> Our new neighbors just moved here from Mexico. Traveling such a long (distence) must be an (aventure.) They have two (countrys) to call home! I was (unabel) to meet their son until school started. We were editing a (notise) about tryouts for the school play, and we both started to make the same (correcshun.)

1. distance **(1 point)**
2. adventure **(1)**
3. countries **(1)**
4. unable **(1)**
5. notice **(1)**
6. correction **(1)**

distance
scariest
adventure
countries
notice
unable
correction
inspect
react
busier
respond
spied
pitied
solid
vulture

Story Time On the lines following the story, write the Spelling Words that complete the story.

Before starting the trip, our leader took time to __7.__ to our questions with expert advice. Then he had to carefully __8.__ each wagon. He also tested each horse to see how it might __9.__ to surprises on the trail. I __10.__ the poor animals pulling the heavy wagons. As the departure neared, everybody was __11.__ than ever. Even after two __12.__ weeks of preparation, we still had plenty of work to do.

It was the leader's job to give a warning if he __13.__ trouble. The first day out, a __14.__ circled overhead and worried us. That, however, was not the __15.__ moment of our trip.

7. respond **(1)**
8. inspect **(1)**
9. react **(1)**
10. pitied **(1)**
11. busier **(1)**
12. solid **(1)**
13. spied **(1)**
14. vulture **(1)**
15. scariest **(1)**

Write a Diary Entry On a separate sheet of paper, finish the story above by writing about the scariest moment on the trip. Use the Spelling Review Words. Responses will vary. **(5 points)**

Assessment Tip: Total **20** Points

Name _____

Choosing Pronoun Forms

Underline the word or words in parentheses that correctly complete each sentence.

1. (<u>We</u>, Us) saw tall buildings in the distance. **(1 point)**

2. (<u>I</u>, Me) thought the lakes were beautiful. **(1)**

3. The town of Canandaigua seemed very busy to (we, <u>us</u>). **(1)**

4. (<u>My mother and I</u>, I and my mother) admired the fine clothes of some of the men and women. **(1)**

5. (<u>They</u>, Them) apparently were local residents. **(1)**

6. (<u>My brother and I</u>, Me and my brother) had trail dust on our clothes. **(1)**

7. My mother cares about the appearance of (my brother and I, <u>my brother and me</u>). **(1)**

8. It was (<u>I</u>, me) who needed her curls straightened. **(1)**

9. (I and my brother, <u>My brother and I</u>) stared at the treats in jars at the general store. **(1)**

10. The clerk sold peppermint sticks to (Joshua and I, <u>Joshua and me</u>). **(1)**

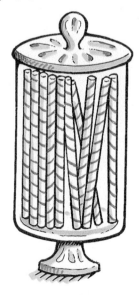

Name _____

Using Pronouns Correctly

Each sentence below has a double subject. Cross out the unneeded subject, and write your new sentence on the line.

1. My uncle ~~he~~ bought some land.

   My uncle bought some land. **(1 point)**

2. The land ~~it~~ was rocky and hilly.

   The land was rocky and hilly. **(1)**

3. Mom ~~she~~ says it's only good for raising sheep.

   Mom says it's only good for raising sheep. **(1)**

4. Sheep ~~they~~ don't mind steep hills.

   Sheep don't mind steep hills. **(1)**

Write either _we_ or _us_ in each blank to correctly complete each sentence.

5. ___We **(1)**___ girls watch the sheep sometimes.

6. The sheep don't always obey ___us **(1)**___ girls.

7. ___We **(1)**___ children always bring uncle's sheepdog with us.

8. The sheep may ignore the shouts of ___us **(1)**___ children, but they cannot ignore the barks and nips of the dog.

182   Theme 5: **One Land, Many Trails**

Assessment Tip: Total **8** Points

Name _____

Autobiography Book Jacket

Use the words in the box to complete the publisher's summary.

The autobiography, written by the famous composer and celebrated violinist Anh Lin, begins with a description of her family and early <u>childhood</u> **(2 points)** experiences. The author shares many early <u>memories</u> **(2)** of her first attempts to play the violin. Lin also reflects on the events that led to her first performance. For the true fan, Anh Lin offers valuable <u>insights</u> **(2)** into the creation of her first musical <u>piece</u> **(2)**. The book even includes lines for violin, flute, and piano from her <u>original</u> **(2)** composition *Autumn Trio.* Her autobiography ends with a description of her <u>present</u> **(2)** musical interests. This is an inspiring and riveting book for music lovers everywhere.

Vocabulary

childhood
insights
memories
original
piece
present

MY MUSIC MY LIFE
by Anh Lin

Assessment Tip: Total **12** Points

Name _____

Life Events Chart

	Langston Terrace	Jane Goodall
Time period	1930s and 1940s **(1 point)**	1930s–1960s **(1)**
Author's age(s) at that time	childhood and teen years **(1)**	childhood through young adulthood **(1)**
Important events, interests, or challenges	• the family's move to Langston • importance of daily life at Langston: enough room, neighborhood games, the library, community spirit **(1)**	• early interest in animals • watching hens lay eggs • took secretarial course and worked for film company • met Leakey in Africa • began study of chimps • got Ph.D. • did research in Tanzania **(1)**
What the events mean to the author	Sample answer: Everyday life at Langston Terrace gave the author a feeling of belonging as she grew up. **(1)**	Sample answer: They all show her interest in animals and her zest for learning. **(1)**
The author's purposes in writing	Sample answer: to pay tribute to a place, to share insights about how place influences a child **(1)**	Sample answer: to share insights about the development of an interesting career **(1)**

What I learned from these autobiographies:

Answers will vary. **(2 points)** _____

_____

_____

Assessment Tip: Total **12** Points

Name _____

Life Experiences

An autobiography helps you learn about other people's experiences. Complete the chart below by writing about an experience that was important to each author in *Focus on Autobiography*. What experience in your life has been important to you? Sample answers shown.

Author	Important Experience
Eloise Greenfield	Moving into Langston Terrace on her ninth birthday is an important event to Eloise Greenfield. She grows to love the community and thinks of it as "a good growing-up place." **(4 points)**
Jane Goodall	Jane Goodall's trip to Africa is an important experience because it leads to her meeting Louis Leakey and getting a job studying chimpanzees. **(4)**
Bill Peet	Bill Peet's experience at a Disney Studios job tryout is important to him. He is excited by being able to work on *Snow White,* the first full-length cartoon film. **(4)**
Alex Rodriguez	Alex Rodriguez's learning experience during his first two years in professional baseball is important to him. He learns how hard athletes need to work to play well. **(4)**
me	Answers will vary. **(4)**

Name _____

How I Was Then . . .

It's the future, and you are famous. A children's magazine has asked you to tell its readers about what was important to you while you were growing up. Write a list of people, places, events, and interests that might be important in your life. Answers will vary.

From My Childhood . . .

People: (4 points) _____

_____

_____

_____

_____

Places: (4) _____

_____

_____

_____

_____

Events: (4) _____

_____

_____

_____

_____

_____

Interests: (4) _____

_____

_____

_____

Assessment Tip: Total **16** Points

Name _____

Life Events Chart

	Bill Peet	**Hit a Grand Slam!**
Time period	1930s **(1 point)**	1990s **(1)**
Author's age(s) at that time	young adult **(1)**	young adult **(1)**
Important events, interests, or challenges	• moves to Los Angeles • tries out and gets job as animator • works on *Snow White* • gets married • enjoys surprise success of the film **(1)**	• learns that pros practice hard • takes part in first major league game • experiences other levels of play and of being a rookie • influence of his mother during the tough times • the joy of a great playoff series **(1)**
What the events mean to the author	Sample answer: They show that a shaky beginning and persistence can lead to success. **(1)**	Sample answer: They reflect his love of the game and his belief in hard work and persistence. **(1)**
The author's purposes in writing	Sample answer: to share interesting memories, to inspire others starting new careers **(1)**	Sample answer: to inspire others to persist through tough times, to share interesting memories **(1)**

What I learned from these autobiographies:

(2 points) Answers will vary.

_____

_____

Prefix/Suffix Match

Choose a prefix or suffix and add it to a numbered word below. Write the new word on the line. Then use five of the words in sentences. (1 point each)

1. school   preschool
2. marine   submarine
3. lone   lonely
4. broken   unbroken
5. courage   discourage
6. fill   refill
7. joy   joyful
8. entertain   entertainment
9. discuss   discussion
10. forgive   forgiveness

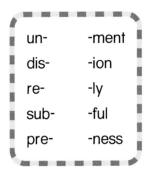

un-	-ment
dis-	-ion
re-	-ly
sub-	-ful
pre-	-ness

Choose five of the new words and use each in a sentence.

11. Answers will vary. _____

12. _____

13. _____

14. _____

15. _____

Name _____

The Sound of *t*

The sound of a final *t* may change to /ch/ or /sh/ when an ending or a suffix is added. Thinking of a related word can help you remember that the /ch/ or /sh/ sound is spelled *t*.

/t/ ➡ /ch/	/t/ ➡ /sh/
fact	locate
factual	location

Write a pair of related Spelling Words in each row. Write each word in the correct column to show whether the final *t* has the /t/, the /ch/, or the /sh/ sound. Underline the final *t* in each word.

Spelling Words

1. fact
2. factual
3. locate
4. location
5. perfect
6. perfection
7. subtract
8. subtraction
9. elect
10. election
11. populate
12. population
13. select
14. selection
15. habit
16. habitual
17. decorate
18. decoration
19. punctuate
20. punctuation

/t/	/sh/
loca<u>t</u>e **(1 point)**	loca<u>t</u>ion **(1)**
perfec<u>t</u> **(1)**	perfec<u>t</u>ion **(1)**
subtrac<u>t</u> **(1)**	subtrac<u>t</u>ion **(1)**
elec<u>t</u> **(1)**	elec<u>t</u>ion **(1)**
popula<u>t</u>e **(1)**	popula<u>t</u>ion **(1)**
selec<u>t</u> **(1)**	selec<u>t</u>ion **(1)**
decora<u>t</u>e **(1)**	decora<u>t</u>ion **(1)**
punctua<u>t</u>e **(1)**	punctua<u>t</u>ion **(1)**

/t/	/ch/
fac<u>t</u> **(1)**	fac<u>t</u>ual **(1)**
habi<u>t</u> **(1)**	habi<u>t</u>ual **(1)**

Name _____

Spelling Spree

Crossword Puzzle **Complete the puzzle by writing the Spelling Words that fit the clues.** (**1 point** for each word)

	Spelling Words
1.	fact
2.	factual
3.	locate
4.	location
5.	perfect
6.	perfection
7.	subtract
8.	subtraction
9.	elect
10.	election
11.	populate
12.	population
13.	select
14.	selection
15.	habit
16.	habitual
17.	decorate
18.	decoration
19.	punctuate
20.	punctuation

Across

2. true
6. capitalize, spell, ___
7. to vote into office
8. something done for a party

Down

1. repeated
3. find
4. 101 − 15 = 86
5. a choice

Suffix Addition or Subtraction **For each word, add or subtract a suffix to write a Spelling Word.**

9. *population* – suffix
10. *locate* + suffix
11. *factual* – suffix

12. *decorate* + suffix
13. *subtract* + suffix

14. *perfect* + suffix
15. *habitual* – suffix

9. populate **(1)** _____
10. location **(1)** _____
11. fact **(1)** _____

12. decoration **(1)** _____
13. subraction **(1)** _____

14. perfection **(1)** _____
15. habit **(1)** _____

Assessment Tip: Total **15** Points

Name _____

Proofreading and Writing

Proofreading **Circle the five misspelled Spelling Words in this excerpt from an autobiography. Then write each word correctly.** Order of answers may vary.

I was so surprised when my best friend, Gus, nominated me for class president, but he believed that I was the (perfec) person for the job. Although I had my doubts, I trusted Gus and agreed to run for the position. Every day after school we were punctual in meeting at the library at 3:00 to work on the campaign. One afternoon Gus helped me make posters. We checked our spelling, capitalization, and (puncuation) carefully. Then he helped me decorate the halls and cafeteria with the posters.

On the day of the (elecshion,) the entire sixth-grade (populatshon) voted to (selecte) a new president. It was a close race, but I won by twenty-eight votes. I'll never forget Gus's faith in me.

Spelling Words

1. fact
2. factual
3. locate
4. location
5. perfect
6. perfection
7. subtract
8. subtraction
9. elect
10. election
11. populate
12. population
13. select
14. selection
15. habit
16. habitual
17. decorate
18. decoration
19. punctuate
20. punctuation

1. perfect **(1 point)**
2. punctuation **(1)**
3. election **(1)**
4. population **(1)**
5. select **(1)**

On a separate piece of paper, write five campaign statements explaining why you should be elected for a class office. Use at least five Spelling Words. (5 points)

Name _____

Names From Places

Read each clue below, and fill in the blank with a word from the box. Beside each word, write the name of the place it comes from. The place name may be the same as the word, or it may be slightly different. You can use a dictionary to check the spelling of the place name. (2 points each)

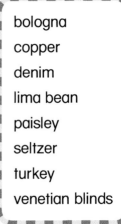

bologna
copper
denim
lima bean
paisley
seltzer
turkey
venetian blinds

1. My name comes from a textile center in southwest Scotland that is known for its colorful patterned shawls.
   paisley, Paisley _____

2. My name comes from a village in central Germany that is famous for its mineral waters. seltzer, Selters _____

3. I am an edible plant, named for a city in Peru where I like to grow.
   lima bean, Lima _____

4. My name comes from a city in north-central Italy, where I was eaten long before I became popular in America. bologna, Bologna _____

5. My name comes from another city in Italy, which is famous for its canals and beautiful architecture. I was actually invented in Japan, not Italy!
   venetian blinds, Venice _____

6. My name comes from a country in southeast Europe and southwest Asia, where I was mistakenly believed to originate. In fact, I'm all American.
   turkey, Turkey _____

Assessment Tip: Total **12** Points

Name _____

My Life in the City

Adjectives with Verbs That Refer to the Senses Use adjectives, not adverbs, with verbs such as *look, feel,* or *hear* when they refer to the senses rather than an action.

>**Adjective:** Todd felt <u>bad</u> after he lost the race.
>**Adverb:** Todd injured his leg <u>badly</u>.

Write the word that completes each sentence correctly.

1. I grew up in the city, and I felt (happy, happily) there.
   happy **(1 point)**

2. I walked to school and observed everything (close, closely).
   closely **(1)**

3. The air smelled (fresh, freshly). fresh **(1)**

4. Car and truck horns sounded (frequent, frequently).
   frequently **(1)**

5. Shopkeepers put out fruit that always looked (ripe, ripely).
   ripe **(1)**

6. The fruit always tasted (sweet, sweetly). sweet **(1)**

7 They felt just (soft, softly) enough. soft **(1)**

8. A kitten jumped up on a table and (quiet, quietly) smelled an orange.
   quietly **(1)**

9. It (gentle, gently) touched some bananas with its front paw.
   gently **(1)**

10. The world looked (beautiful, beautifully) to me. beautiful **(1)**

Name _____

Ragtime Memories

Using *good* and *well* Use the adjective *good* to describe a noun or a pronoun. Remember to use *good* after a linking verb, including verbs such as *look, feel, sound,* or *taste* when they refer to the senses.

Use the adverb *well* to describe an action verb. *Well* is used as an adjective when it refers to health. Do not use *good* when you mean "healthy."

Write *good* or *well* to complete each sentence correctly.

1. My father was a former slave, but he was a (good, well) music teacher.
   good **(1 point)**

2. He always enjoyed (good, well) music. good **(1)**

3. As a child, I was often ill or didn't feel (good, well). well **(1)**

4. My father thought I could be a (good, well) musician. good **(1)**

5. Under his instruction I played several instruments (good, well).
   well **(1)**

6. I was especially (good, well) on the piano. good **(1)**

7. My music was lively, and people thought it sounded very (good, well).
   good **(1)**

8. I felt (good, well) about myself as a musician. good **(1)**

9. I played for audiences, and the performances always went (good, well).
   well **(1)**

10. My success seemed too (good, well) to be true. good **(1)**

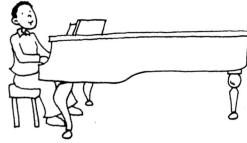

194   Theme 5: **Focus on Autobiography**
Assessment Tip: Total **10** Points

Name _____

My Life with Cars

Using Adjectives and Adverbs Correctly Use proofreading marks to correct seven errors in using adjectives or adverbs to compare, one missing capital letter, three missing or incorrect commas, and one missing end mark in this part of a fictional autobiography of Henry Ford.
(**1 point** for each correction)

Example: I never dreamed I would become one of the ~~more~~ _most_ famous inventor's of the twentieth ℂentury.

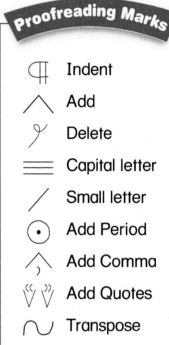

Proofreading Marks

⊔	Indent
∧	Add
૪	Delete
═	Capital letter
/	Small letter
⊙	Add Period
∧	Add Comma
⸌⸍	Add Quotes
∽	Transpose

I was born in 1863. I was interested in automobiles from a very young age‚ I built my first automobile in 1896, and started Ford Motor Company in 1903. I wanted to build a car that many people could buy, but at first my Model T was ~~expensiver~~ _more expensive_ than most people could afford. Our company decided to build cars by using an assembly line‚this made our operation ~~most~~ _more_ productive than it had been. We could sell the cars ~~cheaplier~~ _more cheaply_. Many people wanted to work for me, and I hired the ~~harder~~ _hardest_-working ones.

In the 1920s General Motors was getting a ~~greatest~~ _greater_ market share than Ford. They appealed to more wealthy customers than we did and advertised their cars as ~~luxuriouser~~ _more luxurious_.

In 1932 we manufactured cars with a new V-8 engine. It was the ~~more~~ _most_ powerful engine in any car on the road‚ but we still continued to lose sales to General Motors.

Name _____

Life Events Chart

Use this chart to plan your autobiography chapter. Make notes in the boxes about experiences in your own life.

A Chapter in My Autobiography	
My topic	Anwers will vary. **(2 points)**
Time period and place(s)	**(2)**
My age then	**(1)**
Important events and details	**(5 points)**
What I thought and felt	**(5)**
What this experience means to me now	**(5)**

Assessment Tip: Total **20** Points

Name _____

Writing with Exact Adjectives

Read this paragraph from a draft of an autobiography. Then rewrite it on the lines below, adding adjectives from the list. (You may also add your own adjectives, if you prefer.) Use at least ten adjectives.

Adjectives
fresh
red
long
delicious
clean
rusty
hot
golden
old
rough
gray
bright
green
dirt

Each day I rode my bike down the road to Aunt Lily's house. She was usually waiting on the porch, enjoying the sunshine while she worked. Some days she shelled peas or scrubbed potatoes. Sometimes she peeled apples before she cooked them into pies. She wore her apron, and her hair was braided. She loved farm life, and she passed that love on to me.

Answers will vary; sample answer: Each day I rode my

rusty old bike down the **rough dirt** road to Aunt Lily's

house. She was usually waiting on the porch, enjoying the

golden sunshine while she worked. Some days she shelled

fresh peas or scrubbed potatoes. Sometimes she peeled

bright red apples before she cooked them into **delicious**

pies. She wore her **clean** apron, and her **long gray** hair

was braided. She loved farm life, and she passed that love

on to me. **(10 points)**

_____

_____

Name _____

Animal Encounters

The selections in this theme explore some special relationships between people and wild creatures. After reading each selection, fill in this chart to show what you learned.

	What kind of writing is the selection an example of?	What creature or creatures does the selection describe?
Grizzly Bear Family Book	first-person narrative nonfiction (**2.5 points**)	grizzly bears (**2.5**)
The Golden Lion Tamarin Comes Home	expository nonfiction (**2.5**)	golden lion tamarins (**2.5**)
My Side of the Mountain	fiction (**2.5**)	many small creatures of the forest, such as raccoons and a falcon (**2.5**)

Assessment Tip: Total **10** points per selection and **2** points for the final question

Animal Encounters continued

	What is the purpose of the encounter between humans and animals?	What are the results of the encounter?
Grizzly Bear Family Book	Michio Hoshino wants to learn as much as he can about grizzly bears. He wants to photograph them. **(2.5)**	People learn more about grizzly bears and how they live. **(2.5)**
The Golden Lion Tamarin Comes Home	The people of the Golden Lion Tamarin Conservation Program want to return golden lion tamarins to the forests where they naturally live. **(2.5)**	The golden lion tamarin population increases in the rain forest of Brazil. The monkeys are protected in the preserve. **(2.5)**
My Side of the Mountain	Sam wants to experience the wilderness and be self-sufficient in it. He sees the animals as companions and even friends. **(2.5)**	Sam learns more about himself and about the creatures with whom he shares his woodland home. **(2.5)**

What are some ways in which people can help wild animals? **(2)**

People can help wild animals in zoos learn to live in the wild again. People can

protect wild animals' natural habitats. People can teach others about wild animals

to try to get them to care about the animals and understand their needs.

Assessment Tip: Total **10** Points per selection and **2** points for the final question

Name _____

Creatures of the Far North

Answer each question with a word from the word box.

Vocabulary

carcass
caribou
aggressive
dominance
subservience
tundra
wilderness
abundant
territory
wariness

1. Which word names a grazing animal that lives in the Arctic?
   caribou **(1 point)**
   _____

2. Which word names the frozen land near the Arctic Ocean?
   tundra **(1)**
   _____

3. Which word names land that has not been developed?
   wilderness **(1)**
   _____

4. Which word names the body of an animal that has died?
   carcass **(1)**
   _____

5. Which word is a synonym for *cautiousness*?
   wariness **(1)**
   _____

6. Which word names the region that a predator such as a bobcat or a grizzly bear ranges across to find food?
   territory **(1)**
   _____

7. Which word is an adjective that means "likely to attack"?
   aggressive **(1)**
   _____

8. Which word is an adjective that means "plentiful"?
   abundant **(1)**
   _____

9. Which word means "the state of controlling others"?
   dominance **(1)**
   _____

10. Which word means "the state of being willing to yield to others"? subservience **(1)**
    _____

Assessment Tip: Total **10** Points

Name _____

Detective Work

What generalizations does the author make about bears, about people, and about the wilderness in this selection? As you read, look for generalizations on the pages listed below. Use the clues to help you recognize them. Write each generalization you find.

Page	Clue	Generalization
605	how people see bears	People have a fearful image of bears. **(1)**
607	what all living things do	All living things, including humans, depend on each other for survival. **(1)**
608	how grizzlies act toward each other during most of the year	Grizzlies avoid contact with other bears during most of the year. **(1)**
608	which bears command the best fishing spots	Stronger, more aggressive males usually get the best fishing spots. **(1)**
609	the tolerance of mother bears	Mother bears are usually tolerant of the cubs of others. **(1)**
610	bears selecting salmon	Bears can probably smell the difference between male and female fish. **(1)**
612	bears and soapberries	Bears seem to like soapberries best. **(1)**
614	bears pursuing people	Very few bears are interested in pursuing people. **(1)**
615	how hunters kill bears	A high-powered rifle was fired from a distance. **(1)**
616	how people treat nature	People continue to tame and subjugate nature. **(1)**

Assessment Tip: Total **10** Points

Name _____

Bear Facts

Write facts about bears in the web provided. Try to use each word in the creek at least once.

how bears act with each other

They play; some show dominance; others

show subservience. **(2 points)**

bears and humans

Show wariness toward

each other **(2)**

how bears survive the winter

They sleep in a den. **(2)**

_____

how mother bears act

Show tenderness toward cubs;

tolerant of other bears' cubs; nurse

their young **(2)**

what bears eat

Salmon; sedges; soapberries;

carcass **(2)**

soapberries

carcass

sedges

subservience

nurse

tenderness

salmon

play

dominance

den

wariness

tolerant

Name _____

Wolf Talk

Read the passage. Then complete the activity on page 205.

Saved From Extinction:
The Story of the Gray Wolf

Long ago, the gray wolf roamed through most of North America, from Canada to Mexico. Today, gray wolves are still common in Alaska and parts of Canada. South of Canada, however, only a few gray wolves survive.

People in the United States have always considered wolves to be evil and dangerous. Settlers shot them to protect their families. Ranchers shot them to protect their livestock. For decades the federal government paid hunters cash bounties for shooting wolves.

In the late 1960s, when the gray wolf was nearly extinct in the United States, public opinion began to change. Most people came to regard wolves as a valuable part of the natural environment. All who cared about the wilderness believed that wolves should be allowed to thrive in America's northern forests.

In 1995 federal agencies began a program to return the gray wolf to parts of its former range. They airlifted wolves from Canada into Yellowstone National Park. From there, the wolves have begun to reinhabit parts of Wyoming, Montana, and Idaho. But not everyone is pleased by the program's success. The ranchers in these states fear that wolves will destroy their livestock and have demanded an end to the program.

What will the gray wolf's fate be? No one can be sure. But wherever wolves and people share the land, conflicts are likely to occur.

Name _____

Wolf Talk continued

Answer these questions about the passage on page 204.

1. What generalization does the author make in the second paragraph of the passage?

   People in the United States have always considered wolves to be evil

   and dangerous. **(2 points)**

2. Is this generalization valid or invalid? Why?

   Invalid. It's not true that all people in the United States have always considered

   wolves to be evil and dangerous. **(2)**

3. What two generalizations does the author make in the third paragraph?

   A. Most people came to see wolves as a valuable part of the natural

   environment. **(2)**

   B. All who cared about the wilderness believed that wolves should be

   protected and allowed to thrive. **(2)**

4. One of the generalizations in the third paragraph is invalid. Rewrite it to make it a valid statement.

   Many who cared about the wilderness believed that wolves should be

   protected and allowed to thrive. **(2)**

5. What generalization does the author make in the fourth paragraph?

   The ranchers in these states fear that wolves will destroy their livestock and

   have demanded an end to the program. **(2)**

6. Rewrite the generalization in the fourth paragraph to make it a valid statement.

   Many ranchers in these states fear that wolves will destroy their livestock and

   have demanded an end to the program. **(2)**

Name _____

Prefix Prints

The words in the box begin with the prefix *com-*, *con-*, *en-*,
ex-, *pre-*, or *pro-*. Find the word that matches each clue and
write it in the letter spaces. Then read the tinted letters to
find a word that means "to keep from harm, attack, or
injury."

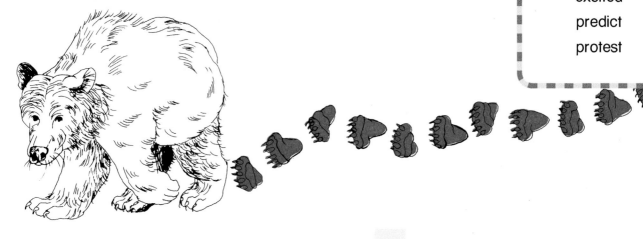

1. bring to a finish   c   o   m   p   l   e   t   e   **(2 points)**

2. a door, for example   e   n   t   r   a   n   c   e   **(2)**

3. to fill with confidence   e   n   c   o   u   r   a   g   e   **(2)**

4. to keep on doing   c   o   n   t   i   n   u   e   **(2)**

5. to tell what will happen   p   r   e   d   i   c   t   **(2)**

6. thrilled   e   x   c   i   t   e   d   **(2)**

7. to complain about   p   r   o   t   e   s   t   **(2)**

Write a sentence about grizzly bears, using a word from the box.
Sample answer shown.

The grizzly bear continued to fish for salmon all afternoon. **(2)**

_____

Assessment Tip: Total **16** Points

More Words with Prefixes

Com-, con-, en-, ex-, pre-, and *pro-* are prefixes. Because you know how to spell the prefix, pay special attention to the spelling of the base word or the word root. Spell the word by parts.

compare   **con**vince   **en**force

excite   **pre**serve   **pro**pose

Write each Spelling Word under its prefix.
Order of answers for each category may vary.

Spelling Words

1. propose
2. convince
3. concern
4. enforce
5. compare
6. excuse
7. conduct
8. preserve
9. contain
10. excite
11. extend
12. prefix
13. engage
14. pronoun
15. consist
16. enclose
17. consent
18. proverb
19. complete
20. exchange

com-, con-

convince **(1 point)**   contain **(1)**

concern **(1)**   consist **(1)**

compare **(1)**   consent **(1)**

conduct **(1)**   complete **(1)**

en-, ex-

enforce **(1)**   engage **(1)**

excuse **(1)**   enclose **(1)**

excite **(1)**   exchange **(1)**

extend **(1)**

pre-, pro-

propose **(1)**   pronoun **(1)**

preserve **(1)**   proverb **(1)**

prefix **(1)**

Name _____

Spelling Spree

Alphabet Puzzler Write the Spelling Word that fits alphabetically between the two words in each group.

1. prong, _____, proof
2. company, _____, compass
3. enchant, _____, encore
4. contact, _____, contest
5. prefer, _____, preheat
6. convert, _____, convoy
7. consider, _____, consonant
8. express, _____, extinct

1. pronoun **(1 point)**
2. compare **(1)**
3. enclose **(1)**
4. contain **(1)**
5. prefix **(1)**
6. convince **(1)**
7. consist **(1)**
8. extend **(1)**

The Third Word Write the Spelling Word that belongs in each group.

9. trade, swap, _____
10. suggest, recommend, _____
11. agree, grant, _____
12. saying, phrase, _____
13. save, protect, _____
14. thrill, energize, _____
15. whole, total, _____

9. exchange **(1)**
10. propose **(1)**
11. consent **(1)**
12. proverb **(1)**
13. preserve **(1)**
14. excite **(1)**
15. complete **(1)**

I really (like, fancy, enjoy) books about bears!

Assessment Tip: Total **15** Points

Name _____

Proofreading and Writing

Proofreading Circle the five misspelled words in these park rules. Then write each word correctly.

PARK RULES

While in the park, please (condouct) yourself as follows:

1. If you see a bear, do not try to (ingage) it. Instead, leave it in peace. Trust us! You don't want a bear to (concirn) itself with you.

2. If you come across a bear, *never* turn and run. It will excite the bear, who will then run after you. There is no way to outrun a bear!

3. Do not feed any park animals. There is no (exscuse) for breaking this rule. We will (enforse) it strictly.

Spelling Words

1. propose
2. convince
3. concern
4. enforce
5. compare
6. excuse
7. conduct
8. preserve
9. contain
10. excite
11. extend
12. prefix
13. engage
14. pronoun
15. consist
16. enclose
17. consent
18. proverb
19. complete
20. exchange

1. conduct **(1 point)**   4. excuse **(1)**

2. engage **(1)**   5. enforce **(1)**

3. concern **(1)**

Write an Essay The author of this selection knew and respected grizzlies, but he was killed by one. Does this change your thinking about bears?

On a separate piece of paper, write a short essay stating your reaction to Michio Hoshino's fate. Use Spelling Words from the list. Responses will vary. **(5)**

Name _____

A Search for Meaning

Read the passage. Then use context clues from the passage to figure out the underlined words. Write their meanings and the clues you used.

Sample answers shown.

The Rivals

Bridget saw the fight through her binoculars. It was really just a brief quarrel between two bears who were fishing. The younger bear was smaller but more aggressive, and he soon proved to be the <u>victor</u>. The older bear turned around and <u>retreated</u> to the riverbank. The entire group of bears in the river then began to fish. The former rivals, now <u>tolerant</u> of one another, fished almost side by side. But Bridget's own feeling of <u>wariness</u> kept her from going any closer.

Word	Meaning	Clues from Context
victor	a winner of a contest **(1 point)**	The bears fought and the younger bear was more aggressive. **(2)**
retreated	went back **(1)**	The older bear turned around and went back to the riverbank. **(2)**
tolerant	accepting **(1)**	The former rivals now fished side by side. **(2)**
wariness	caution **(1)**	It was a feeling that kept her from going any closer. **(2)**

Assessment Tip: Total **12** Points

Name _____

Contraction Action

Contractions with *not* You can combine some verbs with the word *not* to make a **contraction**. An apostrophe takes the place of the letter or letters dropped to shorten the word.

In sentences 1–5, underline the word combination with *not* that can be written as a contraction. Then write the contraction on the line. For sentences 6–10, underline the contraction. On the line, write the words that make up the contraction.

Common Contractions with a Verb and *not*			
do not	don't	have not	haven't
does not	doesn't	has not	hasn't
did not	didn't	had not	hadn't
is not	isn't	could not	couldn't
are not	aren't	would not	wouldn't
was not	wasn't	should not	shouldn't
were not	weren't	cannot	can't
will not	won't	must not	mustn't

1. Bears <u>are not</u> found around here. <u>aren't **(1 point)**</u>

2. I <u>had not</u> seen a bear until last year. <u>hadn't **(1)**</u>

3. I <u>could not</u> visit Alaska. <u>couldn't **(1)**</u>

4. A bear <u>will not</u> show up in my backyard. <u>won't **(1)**</u>

5. I <u>did not</u> think I would ever see a bear. <u>didn't **(1)**</u>

6. "You <u>haven't</u> thought of going to the zoo!" said Dad. <u>have not **(1)**</u>

7. "It <u>isn't</u> the same as seeing wild bears," I said. <u>is not **(1)**</u>

8. He said, "The bears <u>don't</u> live in cages anymore." <u>do not **(1)**</u>

9. The new habitat <u>hasn't</u> been at the zoo long. <u>has not **(1)**</u>

10. You <u>mustn't</u> miss the bear cubs! <u>must not **(1)**</u>

Name _____

No! Not Negatives!

Negatives Words that mean "no" or "not" are **negatives**. Do not use
double negatives, two negative words in the same sentence.

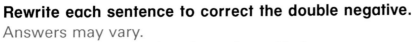

Negatives

no   not   hardly   never   neither   none

There are often two ways to correct a double negative.

   Incorrect: Fred **hasn't no** idea what Alaska is like.

   Correct: Fred **hasn't any** idea what Alaska is like.

   Correct: Fred **has no** idea what Alaska is like.

Alaska

Rewrite each sentence to correct the double negative.
Answers may vary.

1. Fred had not read nothing about Alaska.

   Fred had read nothing about Alaska. OR Fred had not read anything about

   Alaska. **(2 points)**

2. He didn't never plan to go there.

   He didn't plan to go there. OR He never planned to go there. **(2)**

   _____

3. He hadn't no curiosity about our forty-ninth state.

   He hadn't any curiosity about our forty-ninth state. OR He had no curiosity

   about our forty-ninth state. **(2)**

4. Since reading Michio's story, he can't never read enough about Alaska!

   Since reading Michio's story, he can never read enough about Alaska! OR

   Since reading Michio's story, he can't read enough about Alaska! **(2)**

5. Soon there won't be nobody who knows more about Alaska.

   Soon there won't be anybody who knows more about Alaska. or

   Soon there will be nobody who knows more about Alaska. **(2)**

Assessment Tip: Total **10** Points

Name _____

Is That an Adverb, Herb?

Adjective or Adverb? A good writer is careful to use **adverbs**, not **adjectives**, to tell *how much* or to *what extent* about adjectives.

Incorrect: The animal was **dreadful** hungry.

Correct: The animal was **dreadfully** hungry.

Sophie wrote to her friend June. In several places, Sophie used an adjective when she should have used an adverb. Proofread Sophie's letter, and make the corrections above the errors. (2 points each)

Dear June,

    Last week, Mom and I saw a baby raccoon in our yard! It
really
was reat tiny. We knew that it should not be ~~complete~~ completely alone.
terribly
After waiting for its mother for a ~~terrible~~ long time, Mom called

the Wildlife Rescue Center. They sent an expert to help. She was
awfully
~~awful~~ kind. She said we should never touch a wild animal. She

put it in a special cage so it wouldn't get hurt. The Rescue Center
extremely
will take ~~extreme~~ good care of the baby. I wish you could have seen it.
    Your friend,
    Sophie

Name _____

Writing a Paragraph of Opinion

An **opinion** is a belief that may or may not be supported by facts. Some opinions, such as those offered by Michio Hoshino in *The Grizzly Bear Family Book*, are highly personal. For example, he says, "No matter how many books you read, no matter how much television you watch, there is no substitute for experiencing nature firsthand."

As you read *The Grizzly Bear Family Book*, consider the following question:

► *Do you think grizzlies should be kept in zoos? Why or why not?*

Then use this diagram to record your opinion and to write facts and examples that support it. (2 points each)

Opinion

Facts and Examples

Facts and Examples

Facts and Examples

Using the information you recorded in the diagram, write a paragraph of opinion on a separate sheet of paper. In the first sentence, state your opinion in response to the question above. In the body of the paragraph, write two to three reasons why you think and feel the way you do. Support your opinion with facts and examples. Then end your paragraph with a concluding sentence that restates your opinion. (4)

Assessment Tip: Total **12** Points

Name _____

Avoiding Double Negatives

The words *no, not, none,* and *nothing* are called **negatives**. A careful writer does not use two negatives within a single phrase. You can eliminate double negatives in your own writing by removing one of the negatives or by changing either one of the negatives to a positive.

Hunters do **not** have **no** right to shoot grizzlies in Alaska. (incorrect)

Hunters have **no** right to shoot grizzlies in Alaska. (corrected) or
Hunters do **not** have **any** right to shoot grizzlies in Alaska. (corrected)

Read the following letter to the editor of the *Alaskan Argus*. Use the proofreaders' delete mark ( ) to remove double negatives. You may replace some negatives with positive words such as *any* or *anything*. Write the positive word above the negative one you replace. (2 points each)

To the Editor:

I am concerned about a recent proposal to extend the hunting season in Alaska. In my opinion, the hunting season is long enough. Hunters from the lower United States and Europe do not need ̶n̶o̶ *any* more time to hunt.

Most wildlife cannot compete against ̶n̶o̶ high-powered rifles. As a result of more opportunities for hunting animals, there might not be ̶n̶o̶n̶e̶ *any* left for the public to enjoy. Tourists will not come to the Alaskan wilderness if there is ̶n̶o̶t̶ nothing to observe there.

A longer hunting season increases the risk that people will be injured. I feel that if more trophy hunters are encouraged to come to Alaska, then we will not be able to do ̶n̶o̶t̶h̶i̶n̶g̶ *anything* to avoid the tragic consequences.

I strongly support keeping the hunting season the way it is now.

Sincerely,

Chris Morrow

Name _____

Revising Your Persuasive Essay

Reread your persuasive essay. Put a checkmark in the box for each sentence that describes your paper. Use this page to help you revise.

Rings the Bell

☐ My introduction clearly tells my goal.

☐ I supported my goal with at least three important reasons. Facts and details support reasons. I answered objections.

☐ My voice is confident. I used persuasive words.

☐ My paper is organized in paragraphs. My conclusion is strong.

☐ My sentences flow well. There are almost no mistakes.

Getting Stronger

☐ I did not tell my goal clearly in the introduction.

☐ I need more reasons, facts, and details. I did not answer objections.

☐ More persuasive words would make my voice more confident.

☐ Some paragraphs are disorganized. My conclusion is weak.

☐ Some sentences are choppy. There are some mistakes.

Try Harder

☐ My goal is not clear. The introduction is missing.

☐ There are almost no reasons. There are few facts and details.

☐ I don't sound like I care about this goal. Word choice is weak.

☐ My paper has only one paragraph. I didn't write a conclusion.

☐ Most sentences are choppy. There are many mistakes.

Correcting Run-On Sentences

Answers will vary.
Sample answers given.

Correct each run-on sentence on the lines provided.

1. **Run-On:** Wolves are ranked in a pack it is called a hierarchy.

   Corrected: Wolves are ranked in a pack. It is called a hierarchy. **(2 points)**

2. **Run-On:** Lower-ranked wolves are submissive to higher-ranked wolves alpha wolves have dominance over the other wolves in the pack.

   Corrected: Lower-ranked wolves are submissive to higher-ranked wolves, so alpha wolves have dominance over the other wolves in the pack. **(2)**

3. **Run-On:** Wolves survive in different climates they are adaptable.

   Corrected: Wolves survive in different climates because they are adaptable. **(2)**

4. **Run-On:** Wolves hunt in packs they catch larger prey such as moose or elk.

   Corrected: Wolves hunt in packs, and they catch larger prey such as moose or elk. **(2)**

5. **Run-On:** Wolves and dogs share many of the same traits they are both smart.

   Corrected: Wolves and dogs share many of the same traits. They are both smart. **(2)**

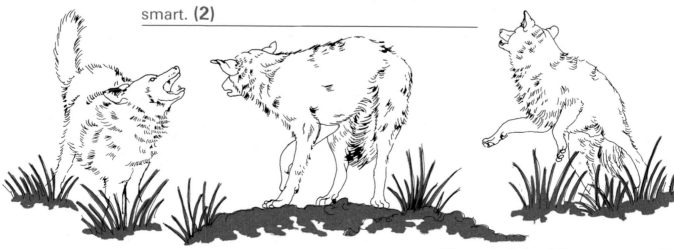

Name _____

Spelling Words

Words Often Misspelled Look for familiar spelling patterns to help you remember how to spell the Spelling Words on this page. Think carefully about the parts that you find hard to spell in each word.

Write the missing letters and apostrophes in the Spelling Words below.

Spelling Words

1. heard
2. your
3. you're
4. field
5. buy
6. friend
7. guess
8. cousin
9. build
10. family
11. can't
12. cannot
13. didn't
14. haven't
15. don't

1. h <u>e</u> <u>a</u> <u>r</u> d **(1 point)**

2. y <u>o</u> <u>u</u> <u>r</u> **(1)**

3. you <u>'</u> <u>r</u> <u>e</u> **(1)**

4. f <u>i</u> <u>e</u> <u>l</u> d **(1)**

5. b <u>u</u> y **(1)**

6. fr <u>i</u> <u>e</u> nd **(1)**

7. <u>g</u> <u>u</u> ess **(1)**

8. c <u>o</u> <u>u</u> <u>s</u> <u>i</u> n **(1)**

9. b <u>u</u> <u>i</u> ld **(1)**

10. fam <u>i</u> ly **(1)**

11. ca <u>n</u> <u>'</u> <u>t</u> **(1)**

12. ca <u>n</u> n <u>o</u> t <u> </u> **(1)**

13. did <u>n</u> <u>'</u> <u>t</u> **(1)**

14. hav <u>e</u> <u>n</u> <u>'</u> <u>t</u> **(1)**

15. do <u>n</u> <u>'</u> <u>t</u> **(1)**

Study List **On a separate piece of paper, write each Spelling Word. Check your spelling against the words on the list.**

Order of words may vary. **(5)**

Assessment Tip: Total **20** Points

Name _____

Spelling Spree

Alphabet Puzzler Write the Spelling Word that fits alphabetically between the two words in each group.

1. fried, _____, frighten
2. head, _____, heart
3. donation, _____, doom
4. familiar, _____, famous
5. guard, _____, guest
6. fiddle, _____, filed
7. button, _____, buzz
8. court, _____, cover

1. friend **(1 point)**
2. heard **(1)**
3. don't **(1)**
4. family **(1)**
5. guess **(1)**
6. field **(1)**
7. buy **(1)**
8. cousin **(1)**

Letter Math Add and subtract letters from the words below to make Spelling Words. Write the new words.

9. carrot + nn – rr =
10. having – ing + en't =
11. sour – s + y =
12. want + ' – w + c =
13. guild – g + b =
14. they're + you – they =
15. hadn't + di –ha =

9. cannot **(1)**
10. haven't **(1)**
11. your **(1)**
12. can't **(1)**
13. build **(1)**
14. you're **(1)**
15. didn't **(1)**

Name _____

Proofreading and Writing

Proofreading Circle the five misspelled Spelling Words in this wanted poster. Then write each word correctly.

HAVE YOU SEEN THIS CAT?

You may have (herd) about the escape of this mountain lion from the county zoo. We have been searching for the past week, but we (have'nt) been able to track her down. Our best (gess) is that she is keeping to wooded areas, but we can't say for sure. As a result, we are asking that you be extremely careful when outdoors, and that you keep an eye on (youre) children and pets. Above all, if you see the cat, (dont) approach her. Instead, call the police, or call us at the zoo at 555-7372.

Spelling Words

1. heard
2. your
3. you're
4. field
5. buy
6. friend
7. guess
8. cousin
9. build
10. family
11. can't
12. cannot
13. didn't
14. haven't
15. don't

1. heard **(1 point)** _____

2. haven't **(1)** _____

3. guess **(1)** _____

4. your **(1)** _____

5. don't **(1)** _____

➤ **Animal Riddles On a separate piece of paper, write three riddles about animals. Include a Spelling Word in each riddle. Then trade riddles with a classmate and try to guess each other's answers.**

Responses will vary. **(5)**

Assessment Tip: Total **10** Points

Name _____

Saving a Species

Complete each statement with a word from the word box.

dilemma
extinction
predator
observation
canopy
reintroduction
habitat
captive
humid
genes

1. If you are in the highest branches of the tallest trees in the rain forest, you are in the canopy **(1 point)**_____ .

2. If the air has a lot of moisture in it, the weather is humid **(1)**_____ .

3. If you release animals into a wild area in which their ancestors once lived, you are helping with the reintroduction **(1)**_____ of a species.

4. If you study the region in which a wild creature lives, you study its habitat **(1)**_____ .

5. If you are faced with a problem that seems to have no good solution, you are faced with a dilemma **(1)**_____ .

6. If you study the material that determines the characteristics of a plant or animal, you study its genes **(1)**_____ .

7. If no members of a species remain alive, that species has suffered extinction **(1)**_____ .

8. If you are being held prisoner, you are a captive **(1)**_____ .

9. If an animal is being watched, it is under observation **(1)**_____ .

10. If an animal hunts other animals for food, it is a predator **(1)**_____ .

Name _____

Get the Idea?

**What are the main ideas of this selection? As you read, find the main
ideas on the pages listed below. Then fill in the chart with the main
idea and the details that support each main idea.** Entries will vary. Samples are
shown.

Topic: The conservation of golden lion tamarins.
(Page 630) Main Idea: The native habitat of the tamarins is a diverse, colorful environment. **(1)**   **Details:** Birds sing, insects buzz, cicadas chirp; tangled vines and leaves; orange-gold flash; speckles of sunlight. **(1)**
(Pages 632–633) Main Idea: Captive-born tamarins need special training before being reintroduced into the wild. **(1)**   **Details:** **(1)**
(Pages 634–637) Main Idea: The observers prepare thoroughly before bringing the tamarins into the wild. **(1)**   **Details:** **(1)**
(Page 638) Main Idea: The observers carefully follow certain steps when releasing the tamarins. **(1)**   **Details:** **(1)**
(Pages 640–641) Main Idea: The observers gradually give less assistance as the tamarins adapt to their environment. **(1)**   **Details:** **(1)**

Assessment Tip: Total **10** Points

Name _____

The Lion Speaks

Fill in the blanks below with information from the story.

1. "I am a <u>golden lion tamarin</u>. My native home is in the rain forest of <u>Brazil</u>." **(2 points)**

2. "Unfortunately, humans have <u>cut</u> down many trees and <u>burned</u> much of the forest for their own use. Today I am in danger of <u>extinction</u>." **(2)**

3. "That is why biologists have established a protected <u>habitat</u> for us in the rain forest. Because many of us are bred in <u>zoos</u>, however, we must learn new <u>skills</u> before we go into the wild." **(2)**

4. "We are trained at the <u>National</u> Zoo in <u>Washington, D.C.</u> Then we are shipped to our native country, <u>Brazil</u>. There a team of <u>observers</u> first releases us into <u>cages</u> within the rain forest." **(2)**

5. "When we are ready, they let us out. They <u>watch</u> us carefully and take detailed <u>notes</u> describing our behavior. They also give us <u>food</u> and <u>water</u> until we learn to find these things on our own." **(2)**

6. "The <u>juveniles</u> among us adapt the fastest. Today only about <u>30</u> percent of us survive more than <u>two years</u> in the wild. The <u>Golden Lion Tamarin</u> Conservation Program hopes to have <u>2,000</u> of us living in the wild by the year <u>2025</u>." **(2)**

Name _____

Mind the Main Idea

Read the passage. Then complete the activity on page 225.

The Decline of the Tiger

Once, many different types of tigers roamed throughout Asia. These were the Indian, Indochinese, Chinese, Siberian, Sumatran, Caspian, Javan, and Balinese tigers. Today, three of these eight types are extinct and several of the others are rare. Wild tigers can still be found only in some parts of Southeast Asia and Siberia.

Two main factors have caused the decline of tiger populations. One factor is the destruction of tigers' habitats. In central Asia, for example, farmers burned wooded areas along waterways to clear the land for farming. Thousands of acres of forest were also set on fire. As a result, much of the tigers' natural prey disappeared. Without enough food to support their roughly four-hundred-pound bodies, the tigers have disappeared as well.

Hunting is the second factor that has caused the decline of tiger populations. With the loss of their habitats and natural prey, tigers began to hunt closer to people. Farmers shot them to protect their livestock. Others hunted them for sport or for their fur.

Today, efforts are being made in many regions to protect wild tigers. India and Nepal have set aside reserves for them. Many countries have outlawed the import or sale of tiger skins. Successful captive breeding programs in zoos are also helping to ensure that the survival of these great cats continues.

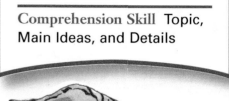

The Golden Lion Tamarin Comes Home

Comprehension Skill Topic, Main Ideas, and Details

Name _____

Mind the Main Idea continued

Answer the questions below. Use information from the passage on page 224. Sample answers are shown.

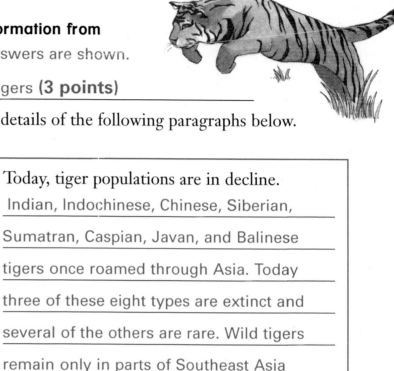

1. What is the topic of the passage? tigers **(3 points)**

2. Write the main idea or supporting details of the following paragraphs below.

First Paragraph	Main Idea:	Today, tiger populations are in decline.
	Supporting Details:	Indian, Indochinese, Chinese, Siberian, Sumatran, Caspian, Javan, and Balinese tigers once roamed through Asia. Today three of these eight types are extinct and several of the others are rare. Wild tigers remain only in parts of Southeast Asia and Siberia. **(4)**
Second and Third Paragraphs	Main Idea:	Two main factors caused the decline of tigers: destruction of their habitats and hunting.
	Supporting Details:	The burning of waterway areas and forests caused the loss of tigers' food sources. Tigers were hunted to protect livestock, for sport, and for their fur. **(4)**
Fourth Paragraph	Main Idea:	Today efforts are being made to save tigers. **(4)**
	Supporting Details:	India and Nepal have set aside tiger reserves. Many countries outlawed importing or selling tiger fur. Zoos breed captive tigers to help more tigers survive.

Assessment Tip: Total **15** Points

Name _____

Syllable Sensations

Read the sentences. Then circle the correct way to divide the syllables of the underlined word. Check the syllable pattern that applies to the word.

	VCV	VCCV
1.	✔ (1)	
2.	✔ (1)	
3.		✔ (1)
4.		✔ (1)
5.		✔ (1)
6.	✔ (1)	
7.	✔ (1)	

1. In zoos, ropes are hung to <u>simulate</u> vines for the tamarins.

   si/mul/ate   (sim/u/late) **(1 point)**

2. Nesting boxes are made for the tamarins from <u>modified</u> picnic coolers.

   mod/if/ied   (mod/i/fied) **(1)**

3. After returning to the rain forest, the tamarins grow <u>accustomed</u> to their new surroundings.

   (ac/cus/tomed) **(1)**   acc/ust/omed

4. As <u>immigrants</u>, the newly arrived tamarins have a great deal to learn.

   imm/ig/rants   (im/mi/grants) **(1)**

5. Human <u>observers</u> watch and record everything the tamarins do.

   (ob/ser/vers) **(1)**   obs/erv/ers

6. Bit by bit, the tamarins become <u>familiar</u> with the rain forest.

   (fa/mil/iar) **(1)**   fam/i/liar

7. Older tamarins must unlearn behaviors that were <u>adequate</u> for zoo life but are useless in the forest.

   a/deq/uate   (ad/e/quate) **(1)**

Assessment Tip: Total **14** Points

Three-Syllable Words

A three-syllable word has one stressed syllable and two syllables
with less stress. To help you spell the word, divide it into its
syllables. Note the spelling of the syllables that have less stress.

va | ca | tion   /vā **kā**′ shən/

ed | u | cate   /**ĕj**′ ə kāt′/

**Write each Spelling Word under the heading that names its
stressed syllable.** Order of answers for each category
may vary.

Stressed First Syllable

dangerous **(1 point)**   regular **(1)**

history **(1)**   natural **(1)**

popular **(1)**   sensitive **(1)**

favorite **(1)**   energy **(1)**

memory **(1)**   period **(1)**

personal **(1)**   property **(1)**

educate **(1)**

Stressed Second Syllable

vacation **(1)**   condition **(1)**

continue **(1)**   imagine **(1)**

potato **(1)**   attention **(1)**

emotion **(1)**

Spelling Words

1. dangerous
2. history
3. vacation
4. popular
5. favorite
6. memory
7. personal
8. educate
9. regular
10. continue
11. potato
12. natural
13. sensitive
14. energy
15. emotion
16. period
17. property
18. condition
19. imagine
20. attention

Assessment Tip: Total **20** Points

Name _____

Spelling Spree

Syllable Scramble Rearrange the syllables to write a Spelling Word. One syllable in each item is extra.

1. ue con gel tin
2. gy ro en er
3. po to tion ta
4. at tion men ten
5. let vor fa ite
6. sen ring tive si
7. u ed gan cate

1. continue **(1 point)**
2. energy **(1)**
3. potato **(1)**
4. attention **(1)**
5. favorite **(1)**
6. sensitive **(1)**
7. educate **(1)**

Spelling Words

1. dangerous
2. history
3. vacation
4. popular
5. favorite
6. memory
7. personal
8. educate
9. regular
10. continue
11. potato
12. natural
13. sensitive
14. energy
15. emotion
16. period
17. property
18. condition
19. imagine
20. attention

Word Maze Begin at the arrow and follow the Word Maze to find eight Spelling Words. Write the words in order.

8. regular **(1)**
9. imagine **(1)**
10. emotion **(1)**
11. dangerous **(1)**

12. personal **(1)**
13. popular **(1)**
14. memory **(1)**
15. vacation **(1)**

Assessment Tip: Total **15** Points

Name _____

Proofreading and Writing

Proofreading Circle the five misspelled Spelling Words in this brochure. Then write each word correctly.

The golden lion tamarin has a sad (histrey.) Over a (perriod) of years, much of Brazil's rain forest was cut down. The tamarin, therefore, was driven out of its (naturel) habitat. Most of the forest was turned into private (propety.) Brazil's government has now set aside some of the remaining forest as a wildlife refuge. Since then, the tamarins' (condishun) has improved. There is still much to be done, however. Won't you help us continue our work?

Spelling Words

1. dangerous
2. history
3. vacation
4. popular
5. favorite
6. memory
7. personal
8. educate
9. regular
10. continue
11. potato
12. natural
13. sensitive
14. energy
15. emotion
16. period
17. property
18. condition
19. imagine
20. attention

1. history **(1 point)**
2. period **(1)**
3. natural **(1)**
4. property **(1)**
5. condition **(1)**

✏️ **Write an Opinion** Only three out of every ten reintroduced tamarins survive for more than two years in the wild. Do you think the time and money spent in this effort is worth it? Why or why not?

On a separate piece of paper, write your opinion of the Golden Lion Tamarin Conservation Program. Use Spelling Words from the list. Responses will vary. **(5)**

Name _____

A Pronounced Difference!

Read the dictionary entries, paying special attention to the pronunciations. Then answer the questions below.

gum
jam
pie
seen
sheen
sit

different /dĭf/ər/ənt/ or /dĭf/rənt/ *adj.* Unlike in form, quality, or nature.

diversity /dĭv/ûr/sĭ/tē/ or /dī/vûr/sĭ/tē/ *n.* 1. Difference. 2. Variety.

program /prō/grăm/ or /prō/grəm/ *n.* A public performance or presentation.

species /spē/shēz/ or /spē/sēz/ *n.* A group of similar animals or plants that are of the same kind and are able to produce fertile offspring.

water /wô/tər/ or /wŏt/ər/ *n.* A compound of hydrogen and oxygen occurring as a liquid.

1. How does the number of syllables change in the two pronunciations of *different*?
   The first pronunciation has three syllables, and the second has two. **(3 points)**

2. *Diversity* differs in pronunciation only in the first **(2)** _____
   two syllables. Which two words from the box have the same vowel sounds as the pronunciations of the first syllable in *diversity*? sit, pie **(2)** ____

3. *Program* differs in pronunciation in the second or last **(2)** _____
   syllable. Which two words from the box have the same vowel sounds as the pronunciations of that syllable? jam, gum **(2)** ____

4. Which word from the box has the same consonant and vowel sounds as the second syllable in the first pronunciation of *species*? sheen **(2)** ____

5. If you use the first pronunciation of *water*, are you saying WAHtur or WAWtur? (Circle the correct answer.) **(2)**

Assessment Tip: Total **15** Points

Name _____

Prepositions Give Positions

Prepositions A **preposition** relates the noun or pronoun that follows it to another word in the sentence. The **object of the proposition** is the noun or pronoun that follows the **preposition**.

Common Prepositions						
about	around	beside	for	near	outside	under
above	at	by	from	of	over	until
across	before	down	in	off	past	up
after	behind	during	inside	on	through	with
along	below	except	into	out	to	without

Underline each preposition and circle the object of each preposition.

1. Sandy visited the rain forest <u>with</u> other (tourists.) **(2 points)**

2. Moisture dripped <u>from</u> the (leaves.) **(2)**

3. The tourists heard bird squawks <u>in</u> the (distance.) **(2)**

4. Sandy took pictures <u>of</u> exotic (orchids.) **(2)**

5. The world would be a poorer place <u>without</u> these (forests.) **(2)**

6. <u>Above</u> our (heads,) we saw howler monkeys. **(2)**

7. Jaguars roam the forest <u>during</u> the (night.) **(2)**

8. We traveled <u>up</u> a (river) <u>to</u> a small (village.) **(2)**

9. The people there made fantastic animal carvings <u>in</u> (wood.) **(2)**

10. I bought a toucan carving <u>from</u> one (artist.) **(2)**

Name _____

Prepositional Phrases Don't Faze Us

Prepositional Phrases A **prepositional phrase** is made up of a preposition, the object of the preposition, and all the words in between.

Write each prepositional phrase on the line.

1. My friend Molly watches birds in her backyard.

   in her backyard **(1 point)**

2. Molly's family lives far from town.

   from town **(1)**

3. In the field wildflowers grow.

   in the field **(1)**

4. Animals leave tracks by the pond.

   by the pond **(1)**

5. The hoots of an owl fill the air.

   of an owl **(1)**

6. Sometimes we camp out in the yard.

   in the yard **(1)**

7. At night stars twinkle in the sky.

   At night, in the sky **(1)**

8. We make out constellations above our heads.

   above our heads **(1)**

9. We tell ghost stories inside the tent.

   inside the tent **(1)**

10. We can hardly sleep during the night.

    during the night **(1)**

Assessment Tip: Total **10** Points

Name _____

Expanding Isn't Demanding

Expanding Sentences with Prepositional Phrases A good writer can make sentences say more by adding prepositional phrases.

 I took a walk.

 Expanded: I took a walk along the path through the woods.

Read Charlie's paragraph. Add details to his description by adding prepositional phrases in the blanks. Ask yourself, Where? When? How? What? Use your imagination!

 Answers will vary. Sample answers shown.

 I walked through the woods <u>in the morning **(1 point)**</u>.

As I walked, I looked <u>at the trees **(1)**</u>. I hoped to see birds,

but they must have been hiding <u>behind the leaves **(1)**</u>. I continued

my walk <u>toward a hill **(1)**</u>. I saw tracks

<u>of an unknown animal **(1)**</u>. I followed them <u>to a stream **(1)**</u>.

<u>At the stream **(1)**</u> I found the owner of the tracks.

It stared <u>at me **(1)**</u>. Not wanting to frighten it, I

stood quietly <u>in the bushes **(1)**</u>. Then it disappeared.

Was it a dream, or did I really see a unicorn <u>in the woods **(1)**</u>?

Name _____

Writing a Compare/ Contrast Essay

In *The Golden Lion Tamarin Comes Home*, you read about similarities and differences between captive-born golden lion tamarins and those born in the wild. Both eat fruit, for example, but golden lion tamarins born in zoos do not know how to hunt or forage for food. One way to explain similarities and differences is by writing a **compare/contrast essay**. Comparing shows how things are alike, and contrasting shows how they are different.

Using the Venn diagram, gather and organize details that compare and contrast grizzly bears with golden lion tamarins. Jot down facts about the two species, including their habitats, their diets, and threats to their survival.

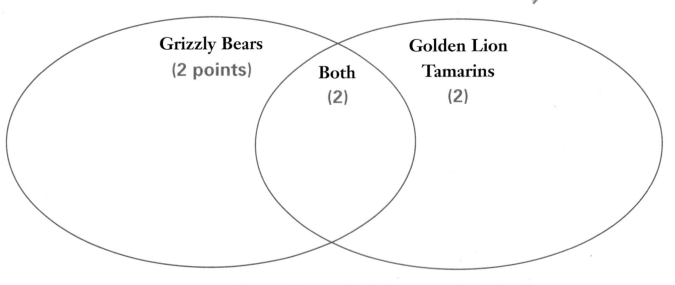

Grizzly Bears
(2 points)

Both
(2)

Golden Lion
Tamarins
(2)

Write a compare/contrast essay about grizzly bears and golden lion tamarins on a separate sheet of paper. In the opening paragraph, clearly state the subject being compared and contrasted. In the following paragraphs, present details from your Venn diagram. Group details that compare and details that contrast in a clear manner. Use clue words such as *both* or *same* to help readers identify likenesses and *in contrast* or *although* to help them identify differences. (4)

Assessment Tip: Total **10** Points

Name _____

Combining Sentences

Good writers are always looking for ways to improve their writing.
One method to streamline your writing is to combine short sentences
that have a repeated subject but differing prepositional phrases into a
single sentence with consecutive prepositional phrases.

The biologist was **in a tropical rain forest.** He stood **beneath
some tall trees.** He peered **into the green vines.** He spotted
a few golden lion tamarins **above him.**

Standing **beneath some tall trees in a tropical rain forest,** the
biologist peered **into the green vines above him** and spotted a few
golden lion tamarins.

**Revise these field notes. Combine short sentences that have a
repeated subject but differing prepositional phrases into a single
sentence. Write the revised notes on the lines.** (12 points)

Thursday, 10:20 A.M.
        My tamarin family, which I call the green team, peeks out. The
monkeys look out from a hole. The hole is in the top chamber. The
chamber is part of a nesting box. One by one, the tamarins leave
the box. Hungrily, the adults poke into the feeder. They probe the
feeder with their long fingers and nails. The golden lion tamarins
also eat some partly peeled bananas. The bananas are left on the
branches. The branches hang near the nesting box.

My tamarin family, which I call the green team, peeks out from a hole in the top

chamber of a nesting box. One by one, the tamarins leave the box. Hungrily, the

adults poke into the feeder, probing with their long fingers and nails. The golden lion

tamarins also eat some partly peeled bananas left on the branches near the nesting box.

_____

Name _____

Late Autumn in the Woods

Complete the paragraph below with words from the word box.

    The leaves have turned colors and fallen from the trees. Most birds have made their <u>migration **(1 point)**</u> south to warmer lands. Farmers have finished <u>harvesting **(1)**</u> the last of the wheat and rye, and they have filled crates with apples and have placed them in a cool <u>storehouse **(1)**</u> . Each squirrel is busy adding a few more nuts to its <u>cache **(1)**</u> of food for winter. Bears gorge themselves on one last meal of berries, for they need to have a thick layer of fat to ensure <u>survival **(1)**</u> through the long winter. The few settlers who have come to the wild lands late in the season hurry to <u>fashion **(1)**</u> shelter that will protect them from the <u>harsh **(1)**</u> weather soon to arrive.

Write three more sentences using words from the box to continue the paragraph.

(3) _____

_____

_____

_____

_____

_____

Assessment Tip: Total **10** Points

Name _____

Use the Clues

**Read the story clues and conclusions provided in the boxes below.
Fill in the missing information with text from the selection.**

Story Clues			Conclusions
pages 652–653 Mice, squirrels, and chipmunks collected seeds and nuts.	+	Sam gathers various roots and smokes fish and rabbit.	=	On the wooded mountain where Sam is living, food is scarce in the winter.
pages 654–655 The animals are growing thick coats of fur and making warm shelters for winter. **(2 points)**	+	Sam realizes he needs to build a small fireplace to warm his shelter. **(2)**	=	Sam's clothing and his current shelter aren't enough to protect him from the cold of winter.
pages 656–658 Sam playfully chases the Baron Weasel up the mountain.	+	Sam runs after Frightful because he is warned the falcon has left him.	=	Sam relies on the animals to keep him from feeling too lonely. **(2)**
pages 660–665 The Baron comes to get food from Sam, but doesn't let him get too close. **(2)**	+	The raccoons make a mess of Sam's food supply. **(2)**	=	Even though Sam enjoys the animals' company, he must remain alert around these wild creatures.

Name _____

Autumn Adventures

The adventures Sam has that are recounted in this story begin in September and end just after Halloween. Use the sequence chart below to write the most important events in the order in which they occurred.

September

Sam watches the coming of autumn. He
gathers roots and tubers and smokes fish and rabbit. **(2 points)**

October 15

The weasel's winter coat, the raccoon's rolls of fat, and the other animals' winter preparations make Sam realize that
he must figure out a way to stay warm in the winter. **(2)**

The next three days

Sam brings clay back to his tree and fashions a chimney. He then
tries several different ways to keep the smoke from going into his home. **(2)**

October 31

After the Baron visits, Sam realizes that it is Halloween. He decides
to put out food so the animals will come to a Halloween party. **(2)**

November 1

The animals finally show up and there is a wild party in which Sam learns that he
must always show the animals that he is the strongest. **(2)**

Assessment Tip: Total **10** Points

Name _____

Gather the Clues

Read the passage. Then answer the questions on page 240.

Taking Stock

It was nearing dusk when I got back to camp. The crickets were just launching into their evening serenade. I set my backpack down on the slab of granite I used as my table and began to unpack the treasures of the day.

I pulled out the sack of miner's lettuce that I'd gathered near the waterfall. Next, I lifted out a pouch of wild blackberries packed in a soft cushion of moss. From the bottom of the pack I drew handfuls of walnuts. The berries I'd expected to find, but the walnuts were an unexpected luxury, from a walnut tree I'd discovered in a grove of tan oaks. I carefully laid the food out on the stone. I had smoked two small trout the day before; these I had wrapped in paper and stored in a tree, away from hungry bears. The trout, nuts, and lettuce, with the berries as dessert, would make a feast indeed.

I then turned my attention to building a fire. The day had been a hot one, but I knew how fast the temperature would drop when the sun went down. After I had the campfire crackling cheerfully, I sat down to take stock.

Some things had gone better than I'd expected. Staying warm and dry had been easy. Even the rainstorm on the second night didn't soak any of my belongings. Other things, like finding enough to eat, had proved harder than I'd expected. An hour of picking lettuce resulted in a very small pile of greens. Overall, though, I couldn't complain. I thought about my two-way radio inside the tent. I hadn't had to use it yet. With luck, I wouldn't need to unpack it at all.

Name _____

Gather the Clues continued

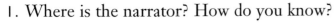

Answer these questions about the passage on page 239.

1. Where is the narrator? How do you know?

   She is in a wilderness area where there are mountains. I can tell because she

   gathers food in the wilderness and camps near a waterfall. **(3 points)**

   _____

2. Is the narrator stranded or did she choose to be there?
   How can you tell?

   She chose to be there. She seems confident and well-prepared. She talks about

   her expectations, so she thought about the trip beforehand. **(3)**

   _____

3. What time of year do you think it is? Why?

   It is summer or close to summer. There are crickets at night, the days are hot,

   and there are fresh berries, nuts, and lettuce. **(3)**

   _____

4. What do you think the two-way radio might be used for?
   Why do you think this?

   I think it might be used to call for help in an emergency. The narrator says she

   hasn't had to use it yet and hopes that she won't have to. **(3)**

   _____

5. Do you think the narrator has had other experiences in the
   wilderness? Why or why not?

   Yes. She knows how to gather food in the wilderness, catch and smoke fish,

   build a fire, and protect her food from bears. **(3)**

   _____

Assessment Tip: Total **15** Points

Name _____

Significant Suffixes

-able, -ible	-ant, -ent
edible	defiant
irresistible	hesitant
climbable	observant
indestructible	tolerant

You are writing a description of *My Side of the Mountain* for your school's Book Week. You need to liven up your description. Use the words from the box above to complete the sentences.

Even when he's angry at them, Sam finds the animals on the mountain <u>irresistible **(2 point)**</u> for the funny things they do. Except for Frightful, he is <u>hesitant **(2)**</u> to get too close to them. Sam tries to be <u>tolerant **(2)**</u> of their bad behavior. But when the Baron Weasel gets that <u>defiant **(2)**</u> look in his eye, watch out!

Sam must prepare a winter shelter that is <u>indestructible **(2)**</u>, even in the worst storm. When out walking, Sam must always be <u>observant **(2)**</u> in order to find <u>edible **(2)**</u> food. He looks for trees that are <u>edible **(2)**</u> so that he can pick the fruit from their high branches.

Name _____

Words with -*ent*, -*ant*; -*able*, -*ible*

The suffixes -*ent* and -*ant* and the suffixes -*able* and -*ible* sound alike but are spelled differently. You have to remember the spellings of these suffixes because they begin with a schwa sound.

| /ənt/ | stud**ent**, merch**ant** |
| /əbəl/ | suit**able**, poss**ible** |

Write each Spelling Word under its suffix.
Order of answers for each category may vary.

-*ent*
different (**1 point**)

student (**1**)

resident (**1**)

absent (**1**)

accident (**1**)

-*ant*
merchant (**1**)

vacant (**1**)

servant (**1**)

-*able*
fashionable (**1**)

comfortable (**1**)

suitable (**1**)

profitable (**1**)

valuable (**1**)

honorable (**1**)

reasonable (**1**)

remarkable (**1**)

laughable (**1**)

-*ible*
possible (**1**)

terrible (**1**)

horrible (**1**)

Spelling Words

1. fashionable
2. comfortable
3. different
4. suitable
5. merchant
6. profitable
7. student
8. possible
9. resident
10. terrible
11. absent
12. vacant
13. servant
14. valuable
15. accident
16. horrible
17. honorable
18. reasonable
19. remarkable
20. laughable

Assessment Tip: Total **20** Points

Name _____

Spelling Spree

Finding Words **Each word below is hidden in a Spelling Word. Write the Spelling Word.**

1. chant __merchant **(1 point)**__

2. sent __absent **(1)**__

3. fit __profitable **(1)**__

4. side __resident **(1)**__

5. rent __different **(1)**__

6. suit __suitable **(1)**__

7. fort __comfortable **(1)**__

Crack the Code **Some Spelling Words have been written in the code below. Use the code to figure out each word. Then write the words correctly.**

8. DHAKHIAP	8.	__valuable **(1)**__
9. URLLSIAP	9.	__horrible **(1)**__
10. BHMUSRFHIAP	10.	__fashionable **(1)**__
11. WPLLSIAP	11.	__terrible **(1)**__
12. MWKOPFW	12.	__student **(1)**__
13. MPLDHFW	13.	__servant **(1)**__
14. URFRLHIAP	14.	__honorable **(1)**__
15. YRMMSIAP	15.	__possible **(1)**__

Spelling Words

1. fashionable
2. comfortable
3. different
4. suitable
5. merchant
6. profitable
7. student
8. possible
9. resident
10. terrible
11. absent
12. vacant
13. servant
14. valuable
15. accident
16. horrible
17. honorable
18. reasonable
19. remarkable
20. laughable

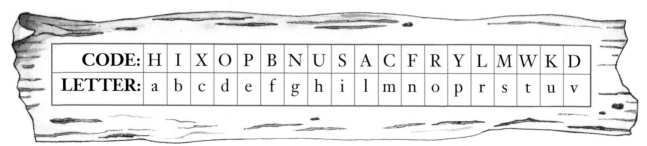

CODE:	H	I	X	O	P	B	N	U	S	A	C	F	R	Y	L	M	W	K	D
LETTER:	a	b	c	d	e	f	g	h	i	l	m	n	o	p	r	s	t	u	v

Name _____

Proofreading and Writing

Proofreading **Circle the five misspelled Spelling Words in this news report. Then write each word correctly.**

Finally tonight, (remarkabel) stories continue

to filter in. We have learned of a wild boy living

on a nearby mountain. Most of the sightings

have been near a (vaccant) farm lot. Town

leaders are dismissing the claims as (laughible.)

Still, as one resident put it, "I don't think it's an

(accidant) that these sightings keep coming in. If

that many people say they've seen him, there's

a (reasenable) chance he's out there."

1. fashionable
2. comfortable
3. different
4. suitable
5. merchant
6. profitable
7. student
8. possible
9. resident
10. terrible
11. absent
12. vacant
13. servant
14. valuable
15. accident
16. horrible
17. honorable
18. reasonable
19. remarkable
20. laughable

1. remarkable **(1 point)**

2. vacant **(1)**

3. laughable **(1)**

4. accident **(1)**

5. reasonable **(1)**

✏ **Write a Character Sketch** Sam Gribley finds food and shelter in the wilderness. He also makes friends with wild animals. What do you think this says about him?

On a separate piece of paper, write a brief character sketch of Sam. Use Spelling Words from the list. Responses will vary. **(5)**

Assessment Tip: Total **10** Points

Name _____

Dictionary Division

**Read the dictionary entries and sentences. On the line after each
sentence, write if the underlined part of the sentence is an idiom or
run-on entry. If it is an idiom, also write what it means. If it is a run-
on entry, also write its part of speech and the main entry word it
belongs with.**

bold *adj.* Having no fear; brave. –**boldly** *adv.* –**boldness** *n.*

clear *adj.* Free from anything that obscures; transparent. –*idioms.* **clear out.** To
leave a place, often quickly. **in the clear.** Free from dangers. –clearly *adv.*
–clearness *n.*

eye *n.* An organ of the body through which an animal sees. –*idioms.* **eye to
eye.** In agreement. **lay (one's) eyes on.** To see.

furious *adj.* 1. Raging. 2. Fierce; violent. –**furiously** *adv.* –**furiousness** *n.*

soft *adj.* Smooth or fine to the touch. –**softly** *adv.* –**softness** *n.*

take *v.* To carry to another place. –*idioms.* **take care.** To be careful. **take off.**
To rise in flight.

1. Sam was sure that Frightful had <u>taken off</u> on a fall migration.
   idiom; risen in flight **(2 points)**

2. In the <u>clearness</u> of the stream Sam could see fish flashing by.
   run-on entry; noun, clear **(2)**

3. As soon as the skunk <u>laid its eyes on</u> Sam, it sprayed.
   idiom; saw **(2)**

4. The squirrels were <u>furiously</u> harvesting nuts.
   run-on entry; adverb, furious **(2)**

5. When Sam shouted, the animals <u>cleared out</u> of his house.
   idiom; left quickly **(2)**

6. Sam kneaded and rubbed the rabbit hides to <u>softness</u>.
   run-on entry; noun, soft **(2)**

Name _____

I Don't Object to Objects

Object Pronouns in Prepositional Phrases Use **object pronouns** as
objects in prepositional phrases.

Object Pronouns	
Singular	**Plural**
me	us
you	you
him, her, it	them

**Underline the pronoun in parentheses that correctly completes
each sentence. (1 point each)**

1. Randy and his dog Maggie came with (I/<u>me</u>) on my walk up Mt.
   Hunter.

2. It seemed to (he/<u>him</u>) that we had found an old farmhouse.

3. We imagined the people who once lived here and told stories about
   (they/<u>them</u>).

4. For (we/<u>us</u>), the old farm was a window into the past.

5. Maggie barked, and we walked toward (she/<u>her</u>).

6. A squirrel in a tree chittered, and Maggie barked at (<u>him</u>/he).

7. More squirrels chittered, and we looked up at (<u>them</u>/they).

8. I guess to (they/<u>them</u>), we were enemies.

9. To (I/<u>me</u>), however, the squirrels were a surprise.

10. We went home. The day had been a success for (we/<u>us</u>).

246   Theme 6: **Animal Encounters**
Assessment Tip: Total **10** Points

Name _____

Pronoun Pronouncements

Pronouns in Prepositional Phrases with Compound Objects Use an object pronoun in a compound object of a preposition. To see whether a pronoun is correct, say the sentence aloud without the other part of the compound.

Underline the pronoun in parentheses that correctly completes each sentence. (1 point each)

1. Lois gave a book about bats to Marjorie and (I/<u>me</u>).

2. We called for Todd and then looked for (he/<u>him</u>) and Adam.

3. Todd stood behind Adam and (I/<u>me</u>) as we looked for bats under the eaves.

4. Lois gave a flashlight to Adam and (we/<u>us</u>).

5. Suddenly, a bat flew in the direction of Adam and (she/<u>her</u>)!

6. Would it fly near Todd and (we/<u>us</u>) too?

7. Marjorie wasn't afraid since she had read the book Lois gave to (she/<u>her</u>) and me.

8. I knew that the bat did not care about Todd or (we/<u>us</u>).

9. Lois did not know that the bat would not fly at the boys or (she/<u>her</u>).

10. The bat flew away, and I gave the book to Todd and (she/<u>her</u>).

Name _____

Pronouns in Compounds

Using the Correct Pronoun in a Compound Structure Good writers are careful to use subject pronouns in compound subjects. They are also careful to use object pronouns in compound objects of a preposition.

Underline incorrect compound subjects and objects in the record below. Then on the lines, write each underlined compound correctly.

June 3, Monday, 4:30 P.M.

     Elizabeth and I walked Princess and Sherlock. Ann arrived to help us. <u>Her and Elizabeth</u> took Sherlock, while I took Princess. Then we met Rick. <u>Him and Ann</u> threw a ball for the dogs.

     We also took care of Lanford the parrot. Elizabeth asked about <u>he and Jackie</u> the parakeet. <u>Elizabeth and me</u> are the bird experts. The birds always have something to say to <u>Elizabeth and I</u>. Today they squawked, "Feathers not fur! Feathers not fur!"

1. She and Elizabeth **(2 points)**

2. He and Ann **(2)**

3. him and Jackie **(2)**

4. Elizabeth and I **(2)**

5. Elizabeth and me **(2)**

248   Theme 6: **Animal Encounters**
Assessment Tip: Total **10** Points

Name _____

Essay Question

An **essay question** is a test question that asks for a written answer of one or more paragraphs. You may write about an experience, give a personal opinion about an issue and back it up with reasons and examples, explain a process, or persuade readers to do or think something.

Circle an essay question that you would like to write about.

A. Explain how Sam Gribley built a fireplace inside a tree by trial-and-error and how he learned from his mistakes in the process.

B. Explain how golden lion tamarins raised in zoos are reintroduced into a wild habitat.

C. Describe an experience you have had in the wilderness or outdoors in which you learned something about yourself.

Organize your answer by filling in the planning chart. First, read the essay question carefully, identifying key words that tell you what kind of answer is needed. Next, jot down main ideas and details you might include. Finally, number your ideas, beginning with _1_, to arrange the order in which you will present them.

Key Words	A. explain how (give steps or reasons)
	B. explain how
	C. describe (give details) **(3 points)**
Main Ideas (3)	
Details (3)	

On a separate sheet of paper, write your answer to the essay question you chose. Begin by restating the question. Then write your main ideas and details in a logical order. (6)

Theme 6: **Animal Encounters**   249
Assessment Tip: Total **15** Points

Name _____

Placing Prepositional Phrases Correctly

Careful writers check the placement of prepositional phrases in their writing. If prepositional phrases appear in the wrong places in a sentence, they can make a sentence unclear. To avoid confusion, place prepositional phrases as close as possible to the words or phrases that they describe.

On a boulder Sam Gribley dried apple slices **in the sun**.

Sam Gribley dried apple slices **on a boulder in the sun**.

Revise the sentences from notes that Sam Gribley might have written. Make the meaning of each sentence clearer by moving one prepositional phrase as close as possible to the word that it describes. Circle the misplaced prepositional phrase, and then draw an arrow to show where it should go. (2 points each)

1. I steered my raft down the creek (with a long stick) to deep pools.

2. (In the icy water) I drifted with my line for an hour.

3. Suddenly the line jerked from my hand (behind the raft.) Dinner!

4. I pulled a fish onto the dry logs (from the blue water) of my raft.

5. Then I pushed (near my home) the raft to the muddy banks.

6. I sprinkled dried herbs on the fresh fish (from a leather pouch.)

7. (Over a fire) I grilled the fish outside my tree for a delicious meal.

Assessment Tip: Total **14** Points

Name _____

Animal Care Words

**Fill in each blank with the Vocabulary word that best
replaces each underlined word or phrase.**

1. Marcus is a <u>doctor who treats sick animals.</u>
   veterinarian **(2 points)**

2. Some animals are calm and obedient during their
   examinations. Other animals are so <u>active</u> their owners must
   be called in to hold them still. feisty **(2)**

3. Most animals are brought into the office for regular checkups. In a
   few cases, Marcus has treated animals with <u>deadly</u> illnesses.
   fatal **(2)**

4. When Marcus suspects that an animal has a broken bone, he takes an
   x-ray. By <u>studying</u> the results, Marcus can tell where the break is and
   how to fix it. analyzing **(2)**

5. When Marcus isn't working at the office, he volunteers at a wildlife
   sanctuary. He believes it is important to help <u>threatened</u> animals.
   endangered **(2)**

> **Vocabulary**
>
> endangered
> veterinarian
> fatal
> analyzing
> feisty

Conclusions Chart

As you read the Paired Selections, use the chart below to draw
conclusions about Kemp's ridley turtles and human beings.
Sample answers are given. Accept reasonable responses.

Interrupted Journey

Details about Kemp's ridley turtles.

Conclusion

| They are endangered. **(1 point)** |

| They can get stranded on beaches. **(1)** |

| Some people know how to care for injured turtles. **(1)** |

| Kemp's ridley turtles need people's help to survive. **(2)** |

The Rabbit's Judgment

Details about human beings.

Conclusion

| They cut down trees to use for wood. **(1)** |

| They make oxen carry heavy loads. **(1)** |

| They kill oxen to use their flesh and hides. **(1)** |

| People use nature in ways that help themselves. **(2)** |

Assessment Tip: Total **10** Points

Name _____

Details Make a Difference

Read the information in the chart below. Write at least two details that support the selected main ideas.

Sample answers are given. Accept reasonable responses.

Interrupted Journey: Saving Endangered Sea Turtles

Main Idea	Supporting Details
page 672C: Max knows what to do when he finds a sick turtle on the beach.	He picks up the turtle and moves it above the high-tide mark to keep it from washing out to sea. He finds seaweed to protect it from the wind. He finds a stick to mark the spot and calls the sea-turtle rescue line of the Massachusetts Audubon Society. **(2 points:** 1 per detail**)**
page 672E: Live turtles can seem to be dead.	Things that might damage the brains of larger animals do not kill turtles. Turtles can survive even when their hearts slow down. A turtle's heartbeat naturally slows down at times in order to save oxygen and keep vital organs working. **(2 points:** 1 per detail**)**

The Grizzly Bear Family Book

Main Idea	Supporting Details
pages 604–605: Mother bears behave similarly to human mothers.	Mother bears play tag with their cubs. They hug their cubs and have fun together. They nurse and care for their cubs the same way a human mother would with her children. **(2 points:** 1 per detail**)**
pages 608–609: Bears create a dominance order when together in a group.	The stronger, more aggressive bears have the best places. When a bear joins a group, there is a brief struggle. Bears try to avoid fighting, but sometimes bears may fight for the higher position. When two bears who have already fought meet again, the loser will give up its place to the winner. **(2 points:** 1 per detail**)**

Theme 6: **Animal Encounters**   253

Assessment Tip: Total **8** Points

Name _____

Decision Words

Write the word from the list that best fits each word or phrase.

1. in a serious and steady way   <u>diligently **(1 point)**</u>

2. state of affairs   <u>situation **(1)**</u>

3. thoughtful decision   <u>judgment **(1)**</u>

4. headed for big trouble   <u>doomed **(1)**</u>

5. thought or feeling   <u>opinion **(1)**</u>

6. thankfulness   <u>gratefulness **(1)**</u>

7. Now write a paragraph about a situation in which you had to make a
   judgment.

   Answers will vary. **(4)**

   _____

   _____

   _____

   _____

   _____

   _____

   _____

Assessment Tip: Total **10** Points

Name _____

Test Practice

Use the three steps you've learned to write a response to this prompt. Complete the chart. Then write your essay on the lines below and on page 256. Use the checklist on page 256 to revise.

Write an essay for your teacher explaining why you like going places with a group of friends. Be sure to include reasons and details.

Use the Revising Checklist to score each student's essay.

Opinion (Answers will vary.)		
Reason	**Reason**	**Reason**
Details	**Details**	**Details**

_____

_____

_____

_____

_____

_____

Continue on page 256.

Theme 6: **Animal Encounters**   255

Test Practice continued

_____

_____

_____

_____

_____

_____

_____

_____

_____

_____

_____

_____

_____

_____

_____

Use another piece of paper if you need to.

Revising Checklist

✔ Does my opinion fit the prompt? Did I state it clearly in the introduction? **(7 points)**

✔ Did I write at least three reasons? **(7)**

✔ Did I write enough details to support each reason? **(6)**

✔ Did I write a separate paragraph for each reason? **(5)**

✔ Did I use exact words? **(5)**

✔ Did I use clear handwriting and correct any mistakes? **(5)**

Read your essay aloud to a partner. Then discuss your answers to the questions on the checklist. Make any other changes that you think are necessary.

Assessment Tip: Total **35** Points

Name _____

Is It Valid?

**Read the generalizations listed below. Then complete the chart.
Look back at *The Rabbit's Judgment* for story details.**

Generalization	Valid? (Yes or No)	Why? (Sample answers shown.)
Hunters always use deep pits to trap tigers.	No **(1 point)**	Not all hunters use deep pits to trap tigers. **(1)**
Most people take pity on animals in danger.	Yes **(1)**	My experience shows that this is true most of the time. **(1)**
People are never grateful for the things they get from nature.	No **(1)**	The word *never* makes this an overgeneralization. Some people are grateful for things from nature. **(1)**
Rabbits that appear in folktales are always clever.	No **(1)**	I've heard and read folktales in which the rabbit is not so clever. **(1)**

Name _____

Adding Up to a Conclusion

Read the questions below. Refer to the Anthology pages below for details to help you answer each question. Then fill in the chart, drawing a conclusion that answers the question. Sample answers shown.

1. Why is the shallow bay a dangerous place for Kemp's ridley turtles? (pages 672B–672C)

Detail	+	Detail	=	Conclusion
For three months, the shallow water is warm. Then it gets cold quickly. **(1 point)**		The cold water in November and December stuns the turtles. **(1)**		If the turtles aren't able to warm up, they will die. **(1)**

2. How large are Kemp's ridley turtles? (pages 672B–672C)

Detail	+	Detail	=	Conclusion
Max searches for a mound about the size of a pie plate. **(1)**		The photos show him holding one of the turtles. **(1)**		A Kemp's ridley turtle is about a foot in diameter. **(1)**

3. Why does Mark mark the spot where he finds the turtle? (pages 672C–672D)

Detail	+	Detail	=	Conclusion
After marking the spot, he and his mother call the sea-turtle rescue line. **(1)**		Less than an hour later, rescuers come to pick up the turtle. **(1)**		He marks the spot so that the rescuers can find the turtle easily and quickly. **(1)**

4. What are the chances of survival of the turtle called Orange? (pages 672D–672G)

Detail	+	Detail	=	Conclusion
The normal body temperature of a Kemp's ridley turtle is about 75 degrees Fahrenheit. **(1)**		Orange has a temperature of 70 degrees Fahrenheit, clear lungs, and a good heart rate, and makes swimming motions, even though his breathing rate is still low. **(1)**		Orange probably has a good chance of surviving. **(1)**

Assessment Tip: Total **12** Points

Name _____

Suffix Sort

Read the sentences. Circle the word in each sentence to which the suffix *-ant, -ent, -able,* or *-ible* has been added. Write the base word and suffix on the line. Then write the word's meaning.

1. Their story was not very (believable.)

   believe, -able; "able to be believed" **(2 points)**

2. Is seaweed (digestible) for turtles?

   digest, -ible; "able to be digested" **(2)**

3. Sometimes monkeys can be quite (approachable.)

   approach, -able; "able to be approached" **(2)**

4. Wolves are the (dominant) species in this area.

   dominate, -ant; "adjective form of dominate" **(2)**

5. The turtles are (dependent) on people for their survival.

   depend, -ent; "adjective form of depend" **(2)**

6. With the help of volunteers, the forests will be (sustainable.)

   sustain, -able; "able to be sustained" **(2)**

Theme 6: **Animal Encounters**   259

Assessment Tip: Total **12** Points

Idioms and Run-on Dictionary Entries

For each entry word below, read the dictionary definitions, idioms, and run-on entries. Then decide whether each numbered sentence uses an inflected form, idiom, or run-on entry. Then tell the meaning of the words or phrases underlined in the sentences below.

> **as** (ăz) *adv.* **1.** Equally. **2.** For instance. —*idiom.* **as is:** Just the way it is, without changes.
>
> **bead** (bēd) *n.* **1.** A small often round piece of glass, metal, wood, etc., having a hole in it through which a string can be drawn. **2.** A small round object, such as a drop of moisture. —*v.* To decorate with beads or beading. —**bead•ed** *adj.* —*idiom.* **draw a bead on.** To take precise aim at.
>
> **bear** (bâr) *v.* bore, borne, bearing. **1.** To hold up; support. **2.** To carry on one's person. **3.** To put up with; endure. —*idioms.* **bear in mind.** To remember. **bear with.** To be patient with.
>
> **beautify** (byo͞o´ təfī) *v.* beautified, beautifying, beautifies. To make beautiful. —**beau•ti•fi•ca'tion** *n.*

1. The shelter took the turtles <u>as is.</u> <u>idiom: just the way they are</u> **(2 points)**

2. She wore a beautifully <u>beaded</u> gown.
   <u>run-on entry: an adjective indicating that the gown has been decorated with beads</u>. **(2)**

3. The beach cleanup was part of an effort toward town <u>beautification.</u>
   <u>run-on entry: noun refers to the process of making the town beautiful.</u> **(2)**

4. The photographer had to <u>bear with</u> unexpected obstacles while waiting to
   photograph the grizzlies. <u>idiom: be patient with</u> **(2)**

5. Michio <u>drew a bead on</u> the mother grizzly with his camera lens.
   <u>idiom: took precise aim at</u> **(2)**

Assessment Tip: Total **10** Points

Name _____

Spelling Review

Write Spelling Words from the list on this page to answer the questions. Order of answers in each category may vary.

1–12. Which twelve words have the prefix *com-*, *con-*, *en-*, *ex-*, *pre-*, or *pro-*?

1. enforce **(1 point)**

2. prefix **(1)**

3. condition **(1)**

4. excite **(1)**

5. consist **(1)**

6. enclose **(1)**

7. proverb **(1)**

8. preserve **(1)**

9. complete **(1)**

10. concern **(1)**

11. propose **(1)**

12. continue **(1)**

13–22. Which ten words have the suffixes *-ent*, *-ant*, *-able*, or *-ible*?

13. remarkable **(1)**

14. accident **(1)**

15. suitable **(1)**

16. vacant **(1)**

17. fashionable **(1)**

18. resident **(1)**

19. possible **(1)**

20. merchant **(1)**

21. terrible **(1)**

22. laughable **(1)**

23–30. Which eight words have letters missing below? Write each word.

23. emo—— emotion **(1)**

24. sensi—— sensitive **(1)**

25. pota—— potato **(1)**

26. ——ural natural **(1)**

27. ima—— imagine **(1)**

28. ——ous dangerous **(1)**

29. ——ation vacation **(1)**

30. reg—— regular **(1)**

Assessment Tip: Total **30** Points

Spelling Words

1. remarkable
2. emotion
3. accident
4. sensitive
5. enforce
6. potato
7. suitable
8. prefix
9. vacant
10. condition
11. excite
12. consist
13. fashionable
14. enclose
15. natural
16. proverb
17. resident
18. possible
19. imagine
20. preserve
21. complete
22. merchant
23. dangerous
24. concern
25. terrible
26. propose
27. laughable
28. vacation
29. regular
30. continue

Name _____

Spelling Spree

Hint and Hunt **Write the Spelling Word that best answers each question.**

1. What word could describe lions and mountain climbing?
   dangerous **(1 point)**

2. What word refers to nature? natural **(1)**

3. What vegetable grows in the ground? potato **(1)**

4. What is a short saying that states an idea or truth?
   proverb **(1)**

5. What do you call a person who dresses in the latest styles?
   fashionable **(1)**

6. What do police officers and principals do with rules?
   enforce **(1)** them

7. What word means "strong feeling"?
   emotion **(1)**

8. What is the word for a person who buys and sells things?
   merchant **(1)**

Spelling Words

1. enforce
2. continue
3. emotion
4. prefix
5. merchant
6. remarkable
7. natural
8. dangerous
9. potato
10. fashionable
11. excite
12. preserve
13. possible
14. terrible
15. proverb

Contrast Clues **Write the Spelling Word that means the opposite of the following words.**

9. not *to bore*, but to excite **(1)**

10. not *to destroy*, but to preserve **(1)**

11. not a *suffix*, but a prefix **(1)**

12. not *impossible*, but possible **(1)**

13. not *ordinary*, but remarkable **(1)**

14. not *wonderful*, but terrible **(1)**

15. not *to stop*, but to continue **(1)**

Assessment Tip: Total **15** Points

Name _____

Proofreading and Writing

Proofreading Circle the six misspelled Spelling Words in this paragraph. Then write each word correctly.

> Before we went on (vacashion,) I tried to (imajine) what animals we might see. First we saw a small bird who was a (residunt) of the rain forest. It lived in a (vakant) hollow tree trunk. We thought it might be (sensative) to noise, so we watched quietly. It was (laffable) how it tried to catch a fly.

1. vacation **(1 point)**

2. imagine **(1)**

3. resident **(1)**

4. vacant **(1)**

5. sensitive **(1)**

6. laughable **(1)**

Spelling Words

1. imagine
2. vacation
3. resident
4. vacant
5. sensitive
6. laughable
7. consist
8. complete
9. enclose
10. concern
11. propose
12. regular
13. suitable
14. accident
15. condition

Half Notes Write Spelling Words to complete these notes.

What does a spider web consist **(1)** of?

If I write down everything I see, my notes will be complete **(1)** .

Should it concern **(1)** me that a snake is sleeping in my tent?

I propose **(1)** that we wake at dawn each day.

At home my regular **(1)** breakfast is cereal, but here I eat powdered eggs. Yuck!

A cold northern region is a suitable **(1)** habitat for a polar bear.

I can't follow the tracks because the condition of the footprints is poor.

I squashed a bug by accident !

If I can enclose **(1** these insects in a cage, I can study them.

✏ ▸ **Write Ideas On a separate sheet of paper, write about an animal you would like to study in the wild. Use the Spelling Review Words.**

Responses will vary. **(5)**

Name _____

Writing Contractions and Correcting Double Negatives

Underline the word combination that can be written as a contraction. Then write the contraction on the line.

1. Kemp's ridley turtles <u>do not</u> do well in cold water. <u>don't **(1 point)**</u>

2. This turtle <u>is not</u> able to swim. <u>isn't **(1)**</u>

3. It <u>has not</u> moved at all. <u>hasn't **(1)**</u>

4. Without help, the turtle <u>would not</u> survive. <u>wouldn't **(1)**</u>

5. Fortunately, this turtle <u>will not</u> die. <u>won't **(1)**</u>

Rewrite each sentence to correct the double negative. Answers may vary.

6. I don't see no turtles.

   <u>I don't see any turtles. **(1)**</u>

7. We haven't looked in none of those clumps of seaweed.

   <u>We haven't looked in any of those clumps of seaweed. **(1)**</u>

8. That turtle isn't moving none of its flippers.

   <u>That turtle isn't moving any of its flippers. **(1)**</u>

9. I haven't never rescued a turtle before.

   <u>I have never rescued a turtle before. **(1)**</u>

10. I don't want to do nothing wrong.

    <u>I don't want to do anything wrong. **(1)**</u>

Assessment Tip: Total **10** Points

Name _____

Choosing Pronouns

Underline the pronoun in parentheses that correctly completes each sentence.

1. After being saved by the man, the tiger circled around (<u>him</u>, he). **(1 point)**

2. I would have walked away from (<u>him</u>, he). **(1)**

3. A tiger would run after (I, <u>me</u>) once he was out. **(1)**

4. Tigers are hunters, and you cannot take chances with (they, <u>them</u>). **(1)**

5. Those animals are dangerous to (<u>us</u>, we). **(1)**

6. The tale is a warning for (<u>me</u>, I). **(1)**

7. My father has told it to (we, <u>us</u>). **(1)**

8. My cousin Noreen enjoys tales told by (he, <u>him</u>). **(1)**

9. My father asked about (<u>her</u>, she) last week. **(1)**

10. My aunt bought a book of folktales for (<u>us</u>, we). **(1)**

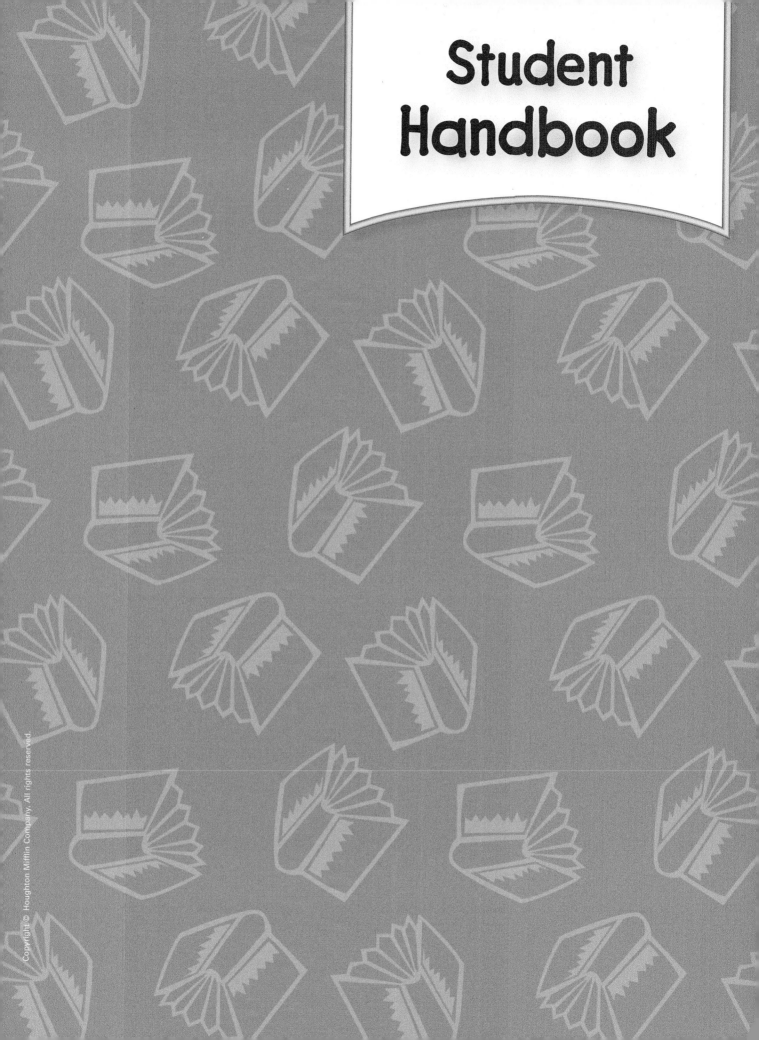

Student Handbook

Contents

How to Study a Word

1. LOOK at the word.
- ► What does the word mean?
- ► What letters are in the word?
- ► Name and touch each letter.

2. SAY the word.
- ► Listen for the consonant sounds.
- ► Listen for the vowel sounds.

3. THINK about the word.
- ► How is each sound spelled?
- ► Close your eyes and picture the word.
- ► What familiar spelling patterns do you see?
- ► Did you see any prefixes, suffixes, or other word parts?

4. WRITE the word.
- ► Think about the sounds and the letters.
- ► Form the letters correctly.

5. CHECK the spelling.
- ► Did you spell the word the same way it is spelled in your word list?
- ► If you did not spell the word correctly, write the word again.

Words Often Misspelled

accept	buy	friend		
ache	by	goes		
again	calendar	going	ninth	tried
all right	cannot	grammar	often	tries
almost	can't	guard	once	truly
already	careful	guess	other	two
although	catch	guide	people	unknown
always	caught	half	principal	until
angel	chief	haven't	quiet	unusual
angle	children	hear	quit	wasn't
answer	choose	heard	quite	wear
argue	chose	heavy	really	weather
asked	color	height	receive	Wednesday
aunt	cough	here	rhythm	weird
author	cousin	hers	right	we'll
awful	decide	hole	Saturday	we're
babies	divide	hoping	stretch	weren't
been	does	hour	surely	we've
believe	don't	its	their	where
bother	early	it's	theirs	which
bought	enough	January	there	whole
break	every	let's	they're	witch
breakfast	exact	listen	they've	won't
breathe	except	loose	those	wouldn't
broken	excite	lose	though	write
brother	expect	minute	thought	writing
brought	February	muscle	through	written
bruise	finally	neighbor	tied	you're
build	forty	nickel	tired	yours
business	fourth	ninety	to	
sy	Friday	ninety-nine	too	

Person to Person
Reading-Writing Workshop

Look for familiar spelling patterns in these words to help you remember their spellings.

Spelling Words

1. a lot
2. because
3. school
4. its
5. it's
6. tonight
7. might
8. right
9. write
10. again
11. to
12. too
13. two
14. they
15. that's

Challenge Words

1. opposite
2. scenery
3. questionnaire
4. excellence
5. pennant

My Study List
Add your own spelling words on the back. ➡

Mariah Keeps Cool

VCCCV Pattern
VCC|CV: laugh|ter
VC|CCV: com|plain

Spelling Words

1. district
2. address
3. complain
4. explain
5. improve
6. farther
7. simply
8. hundred
9. although
10. laughter
11. mischief
12. complex
13. partner
14. orphan
15. constant
16. dolphin
17. employ
18. sandwich
19. monster
20. orchard

Challenge Words

1. control
2. abstain
3. conscience
4. function
5. extreme

My Study List
Add your own spelling words on the back. ➡

Name _____

 My Study List

1. _____
2. _____
3. _____
4. _____
5. _____
6. _____
7. _____
8. _____
9. _____
10. _____

Review Words

1. empty
2. hungry
3. handsome
4. quickly
5. illness

How to Study a Word

Look at the word.
Say the word.
Think about the word.
rite the word.
ck the spelling.

Name _____

 My Study List

1. _____
2. _____
3. _____
4. _____
5. _____
6. _____
7. _____
8. _____
9. _____
10. _____

How to Study a Word

Look at the word.
Say the word.
Think about the word.
Write the word.
Check the spelling.

Dear Mr. Henshaw

Words with Suffixes
safe + ly	= safe**ly**
pale + ness	= pale**ness**
enjoy + ment	= enjoy**ment**
cheer + ful	= cheer**ful**
speech + less	= speech**less**

Spelling Words

1. dreadful
2. enjoyment
3. safely
4. watchful
5. speechless
6. paleness
7. breathless
8. government
9. cheerful
10. actively
11. closeness
12. lately
13. goodness
14. retirement
15. forgetful
16. basement
17. softness
18. delightful
19. settlement
20. countless

Challenge Words

1. suspenseful
2. suspiciously
3. defenseless
4. seriousness
5. contentment

My Study List
Add your own spelling words on the back. ➡

Yang the Second and Her Secret Admirers

Words with *-ed* or *-ing*
deserve + ed	= deserv**ed**
offer + ed	= offer**ed**
rise + ing	= ris**ing**
direct + ing	= direct**ing**

Spelling Words

1. covered
2. directing
3. bragging
4. amusing
5. offered
6. planned
7. rising
8. deserved
9. visiting
10. mixed
11. swimming
12. sheltered
13. resulting
14. spotted
15. suffering
16. arrested
17. squeezing
18. ordered
19. decided
20. hitting

Challenge Words

1. rehearsing
2. shredded
3. anticipated
4. scalloped
5. entertaining

My Study List
Add your own spelling words on the back. ➡

Mom's Best Friend

VV Pattern
V | V
po | em
cre | ate

Spelling Words

1. poem
2. idea
3. create
4. diary
5. area
6. giant
7. usual
8. radio
9. cruel
10. quiet
11. diet
12. liar
13. fuel
14. riot
15. actual
16. lion
17. ruin
18. trial
19. rodeo
20. science

Challenge Words

1. appreciate
2. variety
3. enthusiastic
4. realize
5. eventually

My Study List
Add your own spelling words on the back. ➡

Take-Home Word List	Take-Home Word List	Take-Home Word List

Name _____

 My Study List

1. _____
2. _____
3. _____
4. _____
5. _____
6. _____
7. _____
8. _____
9. _____
10. _____

Review Words

1. title
2. listen
3. wrote
4. finish
5. music

How to Study a Word

Look at the word.
Say the word.
Think about the word.
Write the word.
Check the spelling.

274

Name _____

 My Study List

1. _____
2. _____
3. _____
4. _____
5. _____
6. _____
7. _____
8. _____
9. _____
10. _____

Review Words

1. dancing
2. flipped
3. dared
4. checking
5. rubbing

How to Study a Word

Look at the word.
Say the word.
Think about the word.
Write the word.
Check the spelling.

274

Name _____

My Study List

1. _____
2. _____
3. _____
4. _____
5. _____
6. _____
7. _____
8. _____
9. _____
10. _____

Review Words

1. fearful
2. movement
3. careless
4. lonely
5. powerful

How to Study a Word

Look at the word.
Say the word.
Think about the word.
Write the word.
Check the spelling.

274

One Land, Many Trails
Reading-Writing
Workshop

Look for familiar spelling patterns in these words to help you remember their spellings.

Spelling Words

1. while	9. everybody
2. whole	10. everyone
3. anyway	11. really
4. anyone	12. morning
5. anything	13. also
6. favorite	14. always
7. once	15. first
8. suppose	

Challenge Words

1. embarrass	4. regretted
2. recommend	5. laboratory
3. confidence	

My Study List
Add your own spelling words on the back. ➡

A Boy Called Slow

> **Words with a Prefix or a Suffix**
> PREFIX + BASE WORD:
> **un**able, **dis**cover
> PREFIX + WORD ROOT:
> **in**spect, **re**port
> VERB + *-ion* = NOUN:
> react, reac**tion**
> promote, promo**tion**
> express, expres**sion**

Spelling Words

1. unable	11. react
2. discover	12. reaction
3. report	13. tense
4. disaster	14. tension
5. unaware	15. correct
6. remind	16. correction
7. televise	17. promote
8. television	18. promotion
9. inspect	19. express
10. inspection	20. expression

Challenge Words

1. inquiry	4. except
2. unnecessary	5. exception
3. responsible	

My Study List
Add your own spelling words on the back. ➡

Person to Person
Spelling Review

Spelling Words

1. laughter	17. diary
2. sandwich	18. covered
3. mischief	19. visiting
4. actual	20. govern-ment
5. offered	
6. watchful	21. improve
7. cruel	22. farther
8. planned	23. radio
9. lately	24. fuel
10. countless	25. hitting
11. complain	26. goodness
12. address	27. decided
13. usual	28. actively
14. riot	29. delightful
15. amusing	30. rodeo
16. ordered	

See the back for Challenge Words.

My Study List
Add your own spelling words on the back. ➡

Name _____

 My Study List

1. _____
2. _____
3. _____
4. _____
5. _____
6. _____
7. _____
8. _____
9. _____
10. _____

Challenge Words

1. control
2. extreme
3. rehearsing
4. anticipated
5. defenseless
6. conscience
7. enthusiastic
8. suspenseful
9. entertaining
10. realize

How to Study a Word

Look at the word.
Say the word.
Think about the word.
Write the word.
Check the spelling.

276

Name _____

My Study List

1. _____
2. _____
3. _____
4. _____
5. _____
6. _____
7. _____
8. _____
9. _____
10. _____

Review Words

1. unsure
2. dislike
3. repaint
4. disorder
5. uneven

How to Study a Word

Look at the word.
Say the word.
Think about the word.
Write the word.
Check the spelling.

276

Name _____

My Study List

1. _____
2. _____
3. _____
4. _____
5. _____
6. _____
7. _____
8. _____
9. _____
10. _____

How to Study a Word

Look at the word.
Say the word.
Think about the word.
Write the word.
Check the spelling.

276

Elena

Changing Final _y_ to _i_

army + es = arm**ies**
dirty + er = dirt**ier**
scary + est = scar**iest**
happy + ness = happ**iness**

Spelling Words

1. liberties
2. victories
3. countries
4. spied
5. enemies
6. armies
7. scariest
8. dirtier
9. happiness
10. abilities
11. pitied
12. ladies
13. busier
14. duties
15. lilies
16. worthiness
17. tiniest
18. emptiness
19. replies
20. dizziness

Challenge Words

1. unified
2. levied
3. colonies
4. loveliest
5. strategies

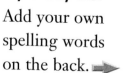

My Study List
Add your own spelling words on the back. ➡

Black Cowboy, Wild Horses

Final /n/ or /ən/, /chər/, /zhər/

/n/ or
/ən/ ➡ capt**ain**
/chər/ ➡ cul**ture**
/zhər/ ➡ trea**sure**

Spelling Words

1. mountain
2. treasure
3. culture
4. fountain
5. creature
6. captain
7. future
8. adventure
9. moisture
10. surgeon
11. lecture
12. curtain
13. pasture
14. measure
15. vulture
16. feature
17. furniture
18. pleasure
19. mixture
20. luncheon

Challenge Words

1. departure
2. leisure
3. architecture
4. texture
5. villain

My Study List
Add your own spelling words on the back. ➡

Pioneer Girl

Unstressed Syllables

voy | age   /**voi**′ ĭj/
na | tive   /**nā**′ tĭv/
no | tice   /**nō**′ tĭs/
dis | tance /**dĭs**′ təns/
for | bid   /fər **bĭd**′/
de | stroy /dĭ **stroi**′/

Spelling Words

1. dozen
2. voyage
3. forbid
4. native
5. language
6. destroy
7. notice
8. distance
9. carrot
10. knowledge
11. captive
12. spinach
13. solid
14. justice
15. ashamed
16. program
17. message
18. respond
19. service
20. relative

Challenge Words

1. adapt
2. discourage
3. cooperative
4. apprentice
5. somber

My Study List
Add your own spelling words on the back. ➡

Name _____

 My Study List

1. _____
2. _____
3. _____
4. _____
5. _____
6. _____
7. _____
8. _____
9. _____
10. _____

Review Words

1. marriage
2. harvest
3. allow
4. package
5. middle

How to Study a Word

Look at the word.
Say the word.
Think about the word.
Write the word.
Check the spelling.

278

Name _____

 My Study List

1. _____
2. _____
3. _____
4. _____
5. _____
6. _____
7. _____
8. _____
9. _____
10. _____

Review Words

1. nature
2. picture
3. capture
4. certain

How to Study a Word

Look at the word.
Say the word.
Think about the word.
Write the word.
Check the spelling.

278

Name _____

 My Study List

1. _____
2. _____
3. _____
4. _____
5. _____
6. _____
7. _____
8. _____
9. _____
10. _____

Review Words

1. cities
2. easier
3. families
4. studied
5. angriest

How to Study a Word

Look at the word.
Say the word.
Think about the word.
Write the word.
Check the spelling.

278

Animal Encounters
Reading-Writing Workshop

Look for familiar spelling patterns in these words to help you remember their spellings.

Spelling Words

1. heard
2. your
3. you're
4. field
5. buy
6. friend
7. guess
8. cousin
9. build
10. family
11. can't
12. cannot
13. didn't
14. haven't
15. don't

Challenge Words

1. truly
2. benefited
3. height
4. believe
5. received

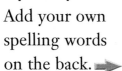

My Study List
Add your own spelling words on the back. ➡

Grizzly Bear Family Book

> **More Words with Prefixes**
> **com**pare **con**vince
> **ex**cite **en**force
> **pre**serve **pro**pose

Spelling Words

1. propose
2. convince
3. concern
4. enforce
5. compare
6. excuse
7. conduct
8. preserve
9. contain
10. excite
11. extend
12. prefix
13. engage
14. pronoun
15. consist
16. enclose
17. consent
18. proverb
19. complete
20. exchange

Challenge Words

1. enactment
2. procedure
3. confront
4. preamble
5. concise

My Study List
Add your own spelling words on the back. ➡

One Land, Many Trails
Spelling Review

Spelling Words

1. unable
2. correction
3. native
4. distance
5. spinach
6. vulture
7. curtain
8. dirtier
9. spied
10. treasure
11. discover
12. inspect
13. tension
14. language
15. respond
16. voyage
17. pleasure
18. countries
19. happiness
20. furniture
21. promotion
22. react
23. solid
24. notice
25. destroy
26. mountain
27. adventure
28. busier
29. pitied
30. scariest

See the back for Challenge Words.

My Study List
Add your own spelling words on the back. ➡

Name _____

 My Study List

1. _____
2. _____
3. _____
4. _____
5. _____
6. _____
7. _____
8. _____
9. _____
10. _____

Challenge Words

1. except	6. architecture
2. apprentice	7. colonies
3. loveliest	8. unified
4. strategies	9. villain
5. inquiry	10. discourage

How to Study a Word

Look at the word.
Say the word.
Think about the word.
Write the word.
Check the spelling.

Name _____

My Study List

1. _____
2. _____
3. _____
4. _____
5. _____
6. _____
7. _____
8. _____
9. _____
10. _____

Review Words

1. compose
2. exact
3. enjoy
4. common
5. expert

How to Study a Word

Look at the word.
Say the word.
Think about the word.
Write the word.
Check the spelling.

Name _____

My Study List

1. _____
2. _____
3. _____
4. _____
5. _____
6. _____
7. _____
8. _____
9. _____
10. _____

How to Study a Word

Look at the word.
Say the word.
Think about the word.
Write the word.
Check the spelling.

Take-Home Word List

Take-Home Word List

Animal Encounters
Spelling Review

Spelling Words

1. excite	16. preserve
2. concern	17. dangerous
3. imagine	18. vacation
4. continue	19. terrible
5. enforce	20. accident
6. propose	21. complete
7. condition	22. regular
8. resident	23. potato
9. possible	24. laughable
10. fashionable	25. remarkable
11. consist	26. proverb
12. prefix	27. natural
13. sensitive	28. emotion
14. suitable	29. merchant
15. vacant	30. enclose

See the back for
Challenge Words.

My Study List
Add your own
spelling words
on the back. ➡

My Side of the Mountain

Words with *-ent, -ant;*
-able, -ible

/ənt/	➡	stud**ent**,
		merch**ant**
/ə bəl/	➡	suit**able**,
		poss**ible**

Spelling Words

1. fashionable	11. absent
2. comfortable	12. vacant
3. different	13. servant
4. suitable	14. valuable
5. merchant	15. accident
6. profitable	16. horrible
7. student	17. honorable
8. possible	18. reasonable
9. resident	19. remarkable
10. terrible	20. laughable

Challenge Words

1. excellent	4. durable
2. prominent	5. reversible
3. extravagant	

My Study List
Add your own
spelling words
on the back. ➡

The Golden Lion Tamarin
Comes Home

Three-Syllable Words

va | ca | tion	➡
/vā **kā**ʹ shən/	
ed | u | cate	➡
/**ĕj**ʹ ə kāťʹ/	
dan | ger | ous	➡
/**dān**ʹ jər əs/	
e | mo | tion	➡
/ĭ **mō**ʹ shən/	

Spelling Words

1. dangerous	11. potato
2. history	12. natural
3. vacation	13. sensitive
4. popular	14. energy
5. favorite	15. emotion
6. memory	16. period
7. personal	17. property
8. educate	18. condition
9. regular	19. imagine
10. continue	20. attention

Challenge Words

1. juvenile	4. amateur
2. astonish	5. obvious
3. ovation	

My Study List
Add your own
spelling words
on the back. ➡

Name _____

 **My Study List**

1. _____
2. _____
3. _____
4. _____
5. _____
6. _____
7. _____
8. _____
9. _____
10. _____

Review Words

1. together
2. beautiful
3. library
4. hospital
5. another

How to Study a Word

Look at the word.
Say the word.
Think about the word.
Write the word.
Check the spelling.

Name _____

 My Study List

1. _____
2. _____
3. _____
4. _____
5. _____
6. _____
7. _____
8. _____
9. _____
10. _____

Review Words

1. current
2. important
3. moment
4. silent
5. parent

How to Study a Word

Look at the word.
Say the word.
Think about the word.
Write the word.
Check the spelling.

Name _____

 My Study List

1. _____
2. _____
3. _____
4. _____
5. _____
6. _____
7. _____
8. _____
9. _____
10. _____

Challenge Words

1. confront
2. preamble
3. astonish
4. excellent
5. reversible
6. enactment
7. juvenile
8. amateur
9. extravagant
10. durable

How to Study a Word

Look at the word.
Say the word.
Think about the word.
Write the word.
Check the spelling.

Focus on Autobiographies

**Consonant Changes:
The Sound of *t***
The sound of a final *t* may change to /sh/ or /ch/ when an ending or a suffix is added.

Focus on Plays

Unusual Spellings
Some words have unusual spellings for vowel and consonant sounds that have to be remembered.

Spelling Words

1. fact
2. factual
3. locate
4. location
5. perfect
6. perfection
7. subtract
8. subtraction
9. elect
10. election
11. populate
12. population
13. select
14. selection
15. habit
16. habitual
17. decorate
18. decoration
19. punctuate
20. punctuation

Spelling Words

1. guy
2. either
3. character
4. machine
5. biscuit
6. scene
7. choir
8. young
9. scent
10. chorus
11. threaten
12. tangerine
13. plaid
14. journal
15. cello
16. scheme
17. southern
18. muscle
19. guarantee
20. typical

Challenge Words

1. exaggerate
2. exaggeration
3. participate
4. participation

Challenge Words

1. schedule
2. dialogue
3. limousine
4. fascinate
5. physical

My Study List
Add your own spelling words on the back. ➡

My Study List
Add your own spelling words on the back. ➡

Name _____

My Study List

1. _____
2. _____
3. _____
4. _____
5. _____
6. _____
7. _____
8. _____
9. _____
10. _____

Review Words

1. blood
2. guest
3. magazine
4. guide
5. type

How to Study a Word

Look at the word.
Say the word.
Think about the word.
Write the word.
Check the spelling.

284

Take-Home Word List

Name _____

My Study List

1. _____
2. _____
3. _____
4. _____
5. _____
6. _____
7. _____
8. _____
9. _____
10. _____

Review Words

1. create
2. creature
3. moist
4. moisture

How to Study a Word

Look at the word.
Say the word.
Think about the word.
Write the word.
Check the spelling.

284

Take-Home Word List

Problem Words

Words	Rules	Examples
bad badly	*Bad* is an adjective. It can be used after linking verbs like *look* and *feel*. *Badly* is an adverb.	This was a <u>bad</u> day. I feel <u>bad</u>. I play <u>badly</u>.
borrow lend	*Borrow* means "to take." *Lend* means "to give."	You may <u>borrow</u> my pen. I will <u>lend</u> it to you for the day.
can may	*Can* means "to be able to do something." *May* means "to be allowed or permitted."	Nellie <u>can</u> read quickly. <u>May</u> I borrow your book?
good well	*Good* is an adjective. *Well* is usually an adverb. It is an adjective only when it refers to health.	The weather looks <u>good</u>. She sings <u>well</u>. Do you feel <u>well</u>?
in into	*In* means "located within." *Into* means "movement from the outside to the inside."	Your lunch is <u>in</u> that bag. He jumped <u>into</u> the pool.
its it's	*Its* is a possessive pronoun. *It's* is a contraction of *it is*.	The dog wagged <u>its</u> tail. <u>It's</u> cold today.
let leave	*Let* means "to permit or allow." *Leave* means "to go away from" or "to let remain in place."	Please <u>let</u> me go swimming. I will <u>leave</u> soon. <u>Leave</u> it on my desk.
lie lay	*Lie* means "to rest or recline." *Lay* means "to put or place something."	The dog <u>lies</u> in its bed. Please <u>lay</u> the books there.

Problem Words continued

Words	Rules	Examples
sit set	*Sit* means "to rest in one place." *Set* means "to place or put."	Please <u>sit</u> in this chair. Set the vase on the table.
teach learn	*Teach* means "to give instruction." *Learn* means "to receive instruction."	He <u>teaches</u> us how to dance. I <u>learned</u> about history.
their there they're	*Their* is a possessive pronoun. *There* is an adverb. It may also begin a sentence. *They're* is a contraction of *they are*.	<u>Their</u> coats are on the bed. Is Carlos <u>there</u>? <u>There</u> is my book. <u>They're</u> going to the store.
two to too	*Two* is a number. *To* means "in the direction of." *Too* means "more than enough" and "also."	I bought <u>two</u> shirts. A squirrel ran <u>to</u> the tree. May we go <u>too</u>?
whose who's	*Whose* is a possessive pronoun. *Who's* is a contraction for *who is*.	<u>Whose</u> tickets are these? <u>Who's</u> that woman?
your you're	*Your* is a possessive pronoun. *You're* is a contraction for *you are*.	Are these <u>your</u> glasses? <u>You're</u> late again!

Proofreading Checklist

Read each question below. Then check your paper. Correct any mistakes you find. After you have corrected them, put a check mark in the box next to the question.

☐ 1. Did I spell all the words correctly?

☐ 2. Did I indent each paragraph?

☐ 3. Does each sentence state a complete thought?

☐ 4. Are there any run-on sentences or fragments?

☐ 5. Did I begin each sentence with a capital letter?

☐ 6. Did I capitalize all proper nouns?

☐ 7. Did I end each sentence with the correct end mark?

☐ 8. Did I use commas, apostrophes, and quotation marks correctly?

Are there other problem areas you should watch for? Make your own proofreading checklist.

☐ _____

☐ _____

☐ _____

☐ _____

☐ _____

☐ _____

☐ _____

Proofreading Marks

Mark	Explanation	Examples
¶	Begin a new paragraph. Indent the paragraph.	¶The boat finally arrived. It was two hours late.
∧	Add letters, words, or sentences.	My friend ate lunch with me today.
℘	Take out words, sentences, and punctuation marks. Correct spelling.	We looked at and admired, the moddel airplanes.
═	Change a small letter to a capital letter.	New York city is exciting.
/	Change a capital letter to a small letter.	The Fireflies blinked in the dark.
⟨⟨ ⟩⟩	Add quotation marks.	Where do you want the piano? asked the movers.
∧	Add a comma.	Carlton my cat has a mind of his own.
⊙	Add a period.	Put a period at the end of the sentence.
∼	Reverse letters or words.	Raed carefully the instructions.
?	Add a question mark.	Should I put the mark here?
!	Add an exclamation mark.	Look out below!

My Notes

Student Handbook

ent Handbook

My Notes